JANE AUSTEN

JANE AUSTEN

HER CONTEMPORARIES AND HERSELF

AN ESSAY IN CRITICISM

BY

WALTER HERRIES POLLOCK

HASKELL HOUSE PUBLISHERS LTD.
Publishers of Scarce Scholarly Books
NEW YORK, N. Y. 10012
1970

First Published 1899

HASKELL HOUSE PUBLISHERS LTD.
Publishers of Scarce Scholarly Books
280 LAFAYETTE STREET
NEW YORK, N. Y. 10012

Library of Congress Catalog Card Number: 73-130248

Standard Book Number 8383-1138-5

Printed in the United States of America

INSCRIBED

TO

F. B. MONEY-COUTTS, ESQ.

AS A SMALL TOKEN OF

SINCERE AFFECTION AND ESTEEM

INTRODUCTION

I CANNOT let this little book go on its way without recording the many thanks I owe to Mr. MONTAGU G. KNIGHT, of Chawton House, great-nephew of Miss Austen, for the invaluable help which he has kindly given me from the beginning to the end of its writing.

W. H. P.

CHAWTON LODGE:
October 1899.

JANE AUSTEN

HER CONTEMPORARIES AND HERSELF

CHAPTER I

So much has been written and so much well written, concerning Miss Austen that there seems to be need for some sort of apology or explanation for putting forth any new volume, however modest, dealing with a writer of gifts and accomplishments which have made her name as famous in the literary world as it was beloved in her family life. These accomplishments and gifts have made for her a monument more lasting than any brass or stone tribute to her memory. Her fame has shone undimmed through all the chops and changes of taste in literature which have flourished and vanished since Sir Walter Scott recorded his generous and well-known appreciation of Jane Austen's powers and of her patient skill in using them. No doubt the quips and cranks and trickeries of literary fashion will go on and on so long as printing is not one of the lost arts; but there will always be many, among whom I count myself one, to believe that Jane Austen's genius will assert itself triumphantly, however many these vacillations and counterchanges in literary taste, and however long they may last.

There is practically nothing, or but trifles, new to be told about Miss Austen's life—a life which one knows to have been the delight of many other lives, and which one likes to believe, with all good ground for the belief, was a source of pleasure to its possessor. It is the aim and intention of the writer to take advantage of such sidelights (many if not most of them thrown by comparison of Miss Austen with other famous women authors just before and just of her own period) as may from time to time present themselves, much as a traveller passing anew over an oft-trodden path may find his attention caught by some combination of light and shade, some tracery thrown through the leaves on to the ground, which gives him an impression hitherto unperceived of a scene well loved and, as he thought, thoroughly well known.

Although nothing could be further from such a purpose than to criticise in any carping spirit the work of former critics and biographers, yet it may be not only permissible but perhaps also not wholly useless to begin by picking up, so to speak, certain threads which have been left loose by previous writers.

Thus, though it is no new pleasure to find myself in accord with that most complete critic, Mr. Austin Dobson, in his high appreciation of Professor

Goldwin Smith's biography—Mr. Dobson speaks of him as 'Miss Austen's most accomplished biographer' —yet there are just one or two little threads to be picked up in Professor Goldwin Smith's most attractive volume ('Jane Austen.' Walter Scott, 1890). On p. 83, for instance, writing of Jane Austen's move, in 1809, from Southampton to Chawton, he says that she 'went to live at a cottage provided by her brother, Edward Knight, close to his residence of Chawton, near Winchester, and not far from Steventon, Jane's old home. Chawton House [and here is Professor Goldwin Smith's slip] has descended to Jane's grand-nephew Lord Brabourne.' This was not so. Miss Austen's second brother, Edward, who on adoption by a rich relative took the name of Knight, became lord of the manor of Chawton. This possession descended to his son, also Edward Knight, and, after, to this second Edward Knight's son, Mr. Montagu G. Knight, the present lord of the manor.

Again, on p. 35 of his excellent biography Professor Goldwin Smith has this remark:

> Perhaps the failure to bring the authors of 'Corinne' and 'Pride and Prejudice' together was not to be deplored, since Madame de Staël pronounced Jane Austen's writings *vulgaires*, by which if she meant anything more than that their subjects were commonplace, she could not have made a less felicitous remark.

Now this, by reason of its saving clause, certainly must not be called a slip. Yet it is worth while to confirm the suggestion embodied in that saving clause. It seems pretty clear from all that is known of Madame de Staël, taken in conjunction with Littré's careful definition of the word *vulgaire*, that what the French author meant was precisely that Miss Austen took her subjects and characters exclusively from every-day life, and in fact that the adjective did not necessarily imply any more dispraise than did Sir Walter Scott's remark that Miss Austen dealt with 'nature in ordinary and middle life'—a statement afterwards repeated by him in the other passage from his diary often quoted, as it is on this very page of Professor Goldwin Smith's work, in high encomium of Miss Austen. One more remark on what again is hardly a slip, if it is a slight error in perception or judgment. On p. 175 we find *à propos* of 'Persuasion :'

> Like Mr. Woodhouse's valetudinarianism, Sir Walter Elliot's conceit is a little overdrawn. He is made to say that he had given somebody a passport to society by being seen with him once in the House of Commons and twice at Tattersall's. If he had belonged either to the House of Commons or to Tattersall's he would have had some of his conceit and insolence knocked out of him. This a woman did not know.

Now, is this quite just to Miss Austen ? If it is unjust, it is certainly a rare occasion on which Professor Goldwin Smith is wanting even by a hair's breadth in appreciation, and yet one cannot but join issue with him on this point, for this following reason. Surely the 'overdrawing' is both very slight and very deliberate, and Sir Walter Elliot's 'conceit and insolence' are intended to be just of that kind which could not be knocked out by any process or experience known to humanity. 'And that's the humour of it.'

While it would be odd indeed if there were any slip as to matters of fact discoverable in the work of one who had such facilities by reason of family connection for becoming acquainted with them as had the first Lord Brabourne (Mr. Knatchbull-Hugessen, grandson of the Edward Austen who became Edward Knight of Chawton House), yet there are in his two-volume book ('Letters of Jane Austen,' with an Introduction and Critical Remarks. Bentley) some matters that may be noticed. Two passages especially, though of no great intrinsic importance, are yet worth a glance for elucidation. On p. 79 of his second volume Lord Brabourne wrote, referring to the letters No. LVI and LVII respectively: 'I cannot pretend to interpret the message sent to "Fanny" respecting the first glee, which is written in a "gibberish" probably only understood by the sender and receiver of the same.' Now 'gibberish' and similar word-tricks are not uncommon institutions and diversions in families of which the members are in constant communication or correspondence, a fact to which Lord Brabourne referred with gravity in his general introduction to the 'Letters' (vol. i. p. 123). Family 'gibberish' is generally manufactured by the transposition or insertion of vowels, consonants, numerals, or all three, and some such schemes of gibberish are not only ingenious, but also at first decidedly puzzling to outsiders.[1] There is, however, little of puzzledom in the messages which Lord Brabourne did not care to unravel. 'The music,' Miss Austen wrote in the first of the two passages, 'was extremely good. It opened (tell Fanny) with Poike de parp pirs praise pof Prapela.' Here it is evident *p* is constantly added, and substituted for other consonants, though, as in the word *praise*, it has no substitute for itself. Leaving alone the puzzle which may be due to misprint or misreading of the manuscript in the words *de* and *pirs*, we arrive, changing *o* to *r* in the first word, at nothing more mysterious than this: 'Strike the harp in praise of Stradella.' (There is one *l* too little in the name.) So again in the subsequent letter—where the gibberish is yet simpler, depending only on the addition or substitution of the consonant *p*, aided by one little misspelling—we have: 'Really, I was never much more put to it than in continuing an answer to Fanny's former message. What is then to be said on the

[1] I remember one such scheme of 'gibberish' used in a family well-known to me, and discovered in a fashion which argued either that the scheme had been hit upon by others, or that the discoverer was a person of keen and trained observation. It happened thus. The scheme was to insert an emphasised *g* before all vowels. Following this scheme, one of two sisters travelling in a railway carriage observed a beautifully carved walking-stick in the hands of an old gentleman sitting opposite, and drew the other sister's attention to it by saying, 'Legook agat hegis stegick'—*look at his stick.* On which the old gentleman, saying 'Would you like to see it nearer?' courteously proffered it for inspection.—W. H. P.

subject? Pery pell, or pare pey? or po; or at the most, Pi, pope, pey, pike, pit.' Now what is this but plainly 'Very well, or dare say, or so (no?); or at the most, I hope they like it'? This deciphering of family gibberish is but a trivial, even puerile, matter in itself, and yet the true students and lovers—the words are synonymous—of Miss Austen's work and life will not, I think, hold it absolutely beneath notice.

Another, and in a way more remarkable, instance of Lord Brabourne's unwillingness to look closely into what is but a very simple matter is found on p. 204 of vol. ii. Miss Austen wrote: 'They [certain patterns of cloth for pelisses] may go from Charing Cross almost any day in the week, but if it is a *ready-money* house it will not do, for the *bru* of *feu* the Archbishop says she cannot pay for it immediately.' On this passage the editor of the Letters has this curious note: 'This expression completely puzzles me. It is clearly written "bru of feu" or "face," and may have been a joke in connection with the fact that "Harriot" was the daughter-in-law of Archbishop Moore, but, if so, the joke is lost.' Well, here Lord Brabourne certainly resembled Homer in that he nodded; for, so far from the joke being lost, there never was any joke to be found or lost. It is simply a question of literally translating Miss Austen's little scrap of French (the habit of French phrases perhaps came, as did the knowledge of private theatricals, from constant companionship, in the Austen home at Steventon, with the young widowed Countess de

Feuillade, daughter of Mrs. Hancock, Jane Austen's aunt). What Miss Austen wrote—using two French words, *bru* and *feu*, for the English words *daughter-in-law* and *the late*—was, 'The daughter-in-law [Harriot] of the late Archbishop says she cannot pay for it immediately.'

This 'Harriot'[1] was Harriet May Bridges, sister to Elizabeth Bridges. Elizabeth Bridges married Edward Austen, who became Edward Knight of Chawton House after her death. Harriet Bridges married George Moore, Rector of Wrotham, and son of '*feu* the Archbishop.' Of Elizabeth Austen there is a miniature by Cosway at Chawton House. It is a fine specimen of Cosway's fine art.

There are some points in Lord Brabourne's volumes which may be conveniently touched on here not for criticism or for clearing up, but merely for remark. Thus, in Letter XI. (Steventon, Nov. 25, 1798) we find mentioned the wearing by a lady of 'what Mrs. Birch would call a *pot hat*'—a piece of slang or cant phrase applied to a woman's hat, curiously antedating the far later identical phrase bestowed on a man's hat. And this reminds one of the like fact that in 'Sense and Sensibility' (chapter lx.) a dance is spoken of as a 'little hop.' But concerning this nomenclature Mr. Austin Dobson points out that

[1] Lord Brabourne apologises for the spelling Harri*o*t, with the words 'My beloved great-aunt was a careless speller.' In fact, Harri*o*t was then quite as correct as Harri*e*t. Cf. Harri*o*t Freke in Miss Edgeworth's *Belinda*.

'nothing is new—even in a novel—and "hop" in this sense is at least as old as "Joseph Andrews."'

Then again (p. 125, vol. ii.) in Letter LXIII., written from her brother Henry's house in Henrietta Street, London, on the evening of September 16 1813, we have this passage: 'We then went to Wedgwood's, where my brother and Fanny chose a dinner set I believe the pattern is a small lozenge in purple, between lines of narrow gold, and it is to have the crest.' This very dinner service is now carefully preserved at Chawton House.

On p. 233 of Lord Brabourne's first volume, in a letter dated Steventon, Saturday evening, Oct. 25 [1800], is a passage which is worth noting on account of one name which occurs in it: 'We have had no letter since you left us, except one from Mr. Serle of Bishopstoke to inquire the character of James Elton,' which at once recalls the inimitable Mr. and Mrs. Elton in 'Emma.' But though Miss Austen, like any other novelist, took names from actual people for her characters, yet it is a thoroughly well-attested fact that in no single instance did she ever draw one of the figures in her novels straight from life. Traits of course from this or that real personage might be recognised, but they were always carefully subdued to and blended with other characteristics, so as to make up a whole personage that could not possibly with any fairness be identified with any one member of the family or society in which she moved. Indeed, as it was not in her style to fall to caricature (*pace*

Professor Goldwin Smith on Sir Walter Elliot), so it was certainly in her character to be scrupulous in avoiding the merest chance of inflicting pain or fostering personal ridicule. And this despite the great probability that she never at all foresaw with what intense curiosity originals for her character-pictures might one day be sought.

Turning to a work by an American 'Austenite' ('The Story of Jane Austen's Life,' by Oscar Fay Adams. Chicago: McClury, 1891), one finds mention of another instance of nomenclature—this time however it is a house, not a person, that is concerned—taken from actual life. On page 161 of a little book of much interest and containing much careful study, Mr. Adams writes, truly enough, that 'it is not at all improbable that the vicinity of Chawton, as an appreciative writer has pointed out, was in the author's mind in several of the descriptions in "Mansfield Park" and "Emma."' Mr. Adams, however, goes on to adopt a curious little slip made by this appreciative writer, Mr. Kebbel, who suggested that 'Chawton House and Chawton Cottage were the models from which Jane drew the stately abode of Sir Thomas Bertram and "The White House," which was the house of the never-to-be-forgotten Mrs. Norris. There is nothing,' says Mr. Adams, 'to offer which very strongly militates against this suggestion.' Well, as far as regards 'The White House' there is, since it stands with name unchanged, plain for all folk to see, on the Selborne Road, and was probably not an infrequent object for a walk when Miss Austen was at Chawton. Again, Mr. Adams quotes Mr. Kebbel's idea that 'Highbury,' where the scene of 'Emma' is laid, 'may have been meant for either Holybourne or Froyle villages, a few miles distant from Alton.' Mr. Adams observes that a likeness may be as easily traced between Highbury and certain Kentish or Somerset villages, and adds that, 'except where existing places were actually named in her books, it is probable that no recognisable description of localities was attempted.' On this it may be remarked that Highbury could not properly be called merely a village. Miss Austen described it as 'a large and populous village, almost amounting to a town.' And it might fairly have claimed the title of a town, since it possessed an inn, the Crown, which contained a ball-room with a card-room adjoining it. Nor can the suggestion about 'recognisable description' be fully accepted, since, from some very palpable hints in 'Emma,' it is obvious enough that Highbury was certainly *not* drawn from the neighbourhood of Alton, which does not lie between 'Mickleham on one side and Dorking on the other' ('Emma,' chapter xlii.), is not in Surrey ('Emma,' chapter xxxii.), nor within Mrs. Elton's 'exploring' distance of Box Hill ('Emma,' chapter xlii.). There is however a place which, though the author has slightly varied the actual geography, corresponds closely enough to the indications just quoted, and is within a mile or so of the distance from London, sixteen miles, which Mr. Frank Churchill covered when he rode to London for the alleged purpose of getting his hair cut, but with the real object of procuring a piano for Jane Fairfax, a lady for whom I personally have found it impossible ever to entertain any strong liking. *Highbury*, the actual name of which may probably have been taken from the London district of that name, is not exactly like *Esher* in its situation, nor perhaps exactly like the Esher of those days in characteristics. But it is certainly more like Esher than any other place according to its description, and Esher certainly was not unfamiliar to Miss Austen, whose uncle by marriage, Mr. Cooper, lived at *Bookham*, hard by, a place of which there is more than one mention in the letters.

Mr. Adams has shown the most laudable painstaking, and has been clear and concise in both his little books (the one not yet mentioned is 'Chapters from Jane Austen.' Boston: Lee & Shepard, 1889). And one must not lightly cavil at an American author who has so deep a veneration for Miss Austen's work and memory. Yet it is not to be denied that this very veneration has led Mr. Adams to strangely underrate the work of some other women novelists, and as strangely to underestimate the repute in which that work is still held.

Her Contemporaries and Herself

CHAPTER II

I ENDED my introductory chapter with a reference to the fact that, as it seems to me, Mr. Adams's affectionate enthusiasm for Miss Austen's work led him to underrate the work of certain other women novelists of a past time. Mr. Adams is by no means the only admirer of Miss Austen whose zeal on her behalf has led him to exalt her as the one woman novelist who shines like a star of the first magnitude among such luminaries as Miss Burney, Miss Edgeworth, and Miss Ferrier, to say nothing of lesser lights. Miss Austen has also been extolled by other admirers as the one woman novelist (*English* understood as previously) who is appreciated alike by men and women. I think it well to go into this matter at once. I must ask leave to begin by stating distinctly that I yield to no one in the deepest and most complete admiration of Miss Austen's work. That very admiration is part reason for my objection not to any exaltation, however far carried, of her very distinct genius, but to the belittling of other writers who had their own touch of genius, in the oddly mistaken idea that such belittling is a kind of tribute to her great qualities. If when several candles are burning in a room you put out all but one, you do not really increase the light given by that one. It is true that for certain stage effects and magic-lantern effects it is necessary to lower all the lights save that which is turned on the object of special interest; but then this is a purely extraneous artificial business, and no one either at work or play was ever less artificial in that sense of the word than Miss Austen. Certainly from all we know of her winning and beautiful nature, of her humility, of her generosity, and of her sense of humour, Miss Austen herself would have been the very first person to resent any attempt at exalting her own merits as a novelist by the process of diminishing the merits of other people. Yet this has constantly been done both in the direct manner of Mr. Adams and in an indirect fashion to be noticed. Mr. Adams certainly does not, as Polonius did, go 'round to work;' there is no beating about the bush with him; no nonsense. Boldly coupling together Mrs. Radcliffe and Miss Burney (what a conjunction!), he as boldly declares that 'curiosity only leads us now to turn to the pages of their books.' As to Mrs. Radcliffe this may be admitted as true, though it is certainly ungrateful, since without Mrs. Radcliffe we should have had no 'Northanger Abbey.' But who save Mr. Adams would venture to assert so roundly that 'we' are impelled only by curiosity to turn to the pages of 'Evelina' and 'Cecilia'? I do not include 'Camilla,' in spite of Miss Austen's own great fondness for it (a matter which might have given pause to Mr. Adams), because, despite its merits, one must not deny that it is long-winded, in some characters grossly overdrawn, and that it certainly misses the astonishing spirit found in 'Evelina' and in the best parts of 'Cecilia.' Not the less is Mr. Adams's 'an honest method' of disposing of Miss Burney's claims to consideration as a novelist, and if not 'as wholesome as sweet' it is most undoubtedly direct. The indirect method referred to above of hiding other people's lights under bushels lest they should interfere with Miss Austen's is a method of indifference and omission. Thus few people who have written concerning Miss Austen have neglected to dwell on Sir Walter Scott's characteristically sincere and kindly praise, which, often quoted as it has been, may be here re-quoted :

> Read again, for the third time at least, Miss Austen's very finely written novel of [1] 'Pride and Prejudice.' That young lady has a talent for describing the involvements of feelings and characters of ordinary life which is to me the most wonderful I ever met with. The big bow-wow strain I can do myself, like any one now going ; but the exquisite touch which renders ordinary commonplace things and characters interesting, from the truth of the description and the sentiment, is denied to me.

Nothing could well be more interesting to students of literature and especially to lovers of Miss Austen's work than such an expression from such a man. But, as has been said, there are other passages of interest

[1] These words for some unaccountable reason are generally omitted in quotation.

referring to Miss Austen and to others in Sir Walter Scott's diary which might well have been compared with this. For instance, in a letter to Miss Joanna Baillie dated Edinburgh, Feb. 10, 1822, Sir Walter Scott wrote:

> I am delighted with the prospect of seeing Miss Edgeworth, and making her personal acquaintance. I expect her to be just what you describe—a being totally devoid of affectation and who, like one other lady of my acquaintance, carries her literary reputation as freely and easily as the milk-maid in my country does the *leglen*, which she carries on her head, and walks as gracefully with it as a duchess. . . . By the way, did you know Miss Austen, authoress of some novels which have a great deal of nature in them?—nature in ordinary and middle life, to be sure, but valuable from its strong resemblance and correct drawing. I wonder which way she carried her pail.

Well, we know with what grace and dignity and modesty Miss Austen 'carried her pail,' but that by the way. On March 29, 1826, Sir Walter Scott made this entry in his diary:

> It [a novel called 'Granby'] is well written, but overlaboured—too much attempt to put the reader exactly up to the thoughts and sentiments of the parties. The women do this better: Edgeworth, Ferrier, Austen, have all given portraits of real society, far superior to anything man, vain man, has produced of the like nature.

Again, Lockhart records a conversation with Sir Walter Scott, then in failing health, at Malta in December 1831:

Among other talk, in returning, he spoke with praise of Miss Ferrier as a novelist, and then with still higher praise of Miss Austen. Of the latter he said, 'I find myself every now and then with one of her books in my hand. There's a finishing-off in some of her scenes that is really quite above everybody else. And there's that Irish lady, too—but I forget everybody's name now'—'Miss Edgeworth,' I said—'Ay, Miss Edgeworth—she's *very* clever, and best in the little touches too. I'm sure in that children's story'—(he meant 'Simple Susan')—'where the little girl parts with her lamb, and the little boy brings it back to her again, there's nothing for it but just to put down the book and cry.'

But Sir Walter Scott paid a higher tribute to Miss Edgeworth than can be found in his Diary or recorded talk, in the General Preface to the Waverley Novels:

Two circumstances in particular recalled my recollection of the mislaid manuscript. The first was the extended and well-merited fame of Miss Edgeworth, whose Irish characters have gone so far to make the English familiar with the character of their gay and kind-hearted neighbours of Ireland, that she may be truly said to have done more towards completing the Union than perhaps all the legislative enactments by which it has been followed up.

Without being so presumptuous as to hope to emulate the rich humour, pathetic tenderness, and admirable tact, which pervade the works of my accomplished friend, I felt that something might be attempted for my own country of the same kind with that which Miss Edgeworth so fortunately achieved for Ireland—something which might introduce her natives to those of the sister kingdom in a more favourable light than they had been placed hitherto, and tend to procure sympathy for their virtues and indulgence for their foibles.[1]

The only passage in the Diary (November, 1826) concerning Madame D'Arblay (Miss Burney) is written with the obvious assumption that the genius of 'Evelina' is too completely recognised to need any comment:

Was introduced by Rogers to Mad. D'Arblay, the celebrated authoress of Evelina and Cecilia—an elderly lady, with no remains of personal beauty, but with a simple and gentle manner, a pleasing expression of countenance, and apparently quick feelings. She told me she had wished to see two persons—myself, of course, being one, the other George Canning. This was really a compliment to be pleased with—a nice little handsome pat of butter made up by a 'neat-handed Phillis' of a dairy-maid, instead of the grease, fit only for cart-wheels, with which one is dosed by the pound.

The diarist went on to note how Madame D'Arblay told the story of Dr. Johnson saying, in Dr. Burney's presence, to Mrs. Thrale, 'You should read this new work, madam—you should read Evelina; every one says it is excellent, and they are right.' He continued:

Mad. D'Arblay said she was wild with joy at this decisive evidence of her literary success, and that she could

[1] Cf. the statement made by an author of a later time—the great Russian novelist Turgenief—that he was an unconscious disciple of Miss Edgeworth in setting out on his literary career. 'It is possible, nay probable, that if Maria Edgeworth had not written about the poor Irish of County Longford and the squires and squireens it would not have occurred to me to give a literary form to my impressions about the classes parallel to them in Russia.'

only give vent to her rapture by dancing and skipping round a mulberry-tree in the garden. She was very young at this time.[1] I trust I shall see this lady again.

Johnson's admiration of 'Evelina' and 'Cecilia' ('Sir, if you talk of Cecilia, talk on') is well known, and in Miss Annie Raine Ellis's Introduction to 'Evelina' we are reminded of the great Burke's 'noble excess' in the enthusiastic 'One book of hers is equal to a thousand of others.'

It would not be difficult to find more instances of evidence that the women-authors referred to (Miss Burney at the head of them, but to be sure she came first) were assigned places in the very first rank of novelists by the very finest critics of their times. Enough has been presented, some may think more than enough, for the special purpose which has led to the foregoing quotations. Readers may already have asked themselves 'Why all this pother about Miss Burney, Miss Edgeworth, Miss Ferrier, in a book devoted to Miss Austen?' Well, the answer is simple enough, or rather I should say the answers. The first reply is contained in what has been said before—that Miss Austen herself would have been the very first to deplore any indifference to, any neglect of, her compeers exhibited, by a foolish blunder, as a means of giving added brilliancy to her own genius, which assuredly needs no artificial

[1] The exact age of Miss Burney when she wrote *Evelina* cannot be ascertained. Croker's decidedly malevolent remarks on the matter, and Macaulay's cutting retort will be remembered.

setting-off. The second reason is more complex and it may be more practical. There are enthusiasts for Miss Austen, and Heaven forbid one should discourage such enthusiasm in itself, who, like Mr. Adams, ignore, wilfully or not, the fact that Miss Burney is still read and admired for motives far different from curiosity. The same class of enthusiast would doubtless ignore Miss Edgeworth and Miss Ferrier, who maybe, 'taking it by and large,' are now a good deal less read than Miss Burney and certainly a great deal less read than Miss Austen. There are real lovers of literature who are content with their reminiscences, refreshed perhaps by an occasional dip into the volumes they once knew well, of the three authors mentioned, while they turn again and again not only to the pages but actually to the books of Miss Austen. And it is not my concern to deny that one can read, say, 'Emma' with perfect satisfaction right through several times, while one might be content with re-reading 'Evelina' once, with accustomed 'skippings.' And again there are lovers and students of literature who, fully recognising the genius of the other writers, feel something of the same greater attraction in Miss Austen's work which leads to an easy and oft-repeated recurrence to it for pure delight in reading.

Now as these things are so, and I do not think it will be denied that they are so, may it not be worth while to go a little deeper into the question? To try to ascertain why it is that

Miss Austen's star outshines the others? It is a voyage of discovery, but one that seems worth undertaking. It was necessary to show how bright were the other stars before embarking on such an enterprise. Having shown this, I propose, with, I trust, becoming humility, to attempt that adventure.

Jane Austen

CHAPTER III

It is not a matter of very great difficulty to find merely general explanation of the facts that Miss Austen's place is unique among women novelists and that her work is read more constantly and with completer pleasure by natural and by trained critics than that of the other authors who have been named, while it is known and loved by many readers of taste who may know little or really nothing of such work and who certainly do not greatly affect it. For one thing, Miss Austen—an artist, consciously or not, to the tips of her fingers—knew exactly, it would seem, the limitations of her own powers and never made an excursion into realms beyond those in which the usual occurrences of a life where there is no room for hairbreadth 'scapes have their place. And on that hangs another reason for particular popularity—if a contradiction in terms may be allowed. This reason will be found in the following extract from Sir Walter Scott's article in No. xxvii. of the 'Quarterly Review.' It is worth noting by the way that his favourites among her novels were, according to Lockhart, 'Emma' and 'Northanger Abbey.'

We bestow no mean compliment upon the author of 'Emma' when we say that keeping close to common incidents, and to such characters as occupy the ordinary walks of life, she has produced sketches of such spirit and originality, that we never miss the excitation which depends upon a narrative of uncommon events, arising from the consideration of minds, manners, and sentiments, greatly above our own. In this class she stands almost alone; for the scenes of Miss Edgeworth are laid in higher life, varied by more romantic incident, and by her remarkable power of embodying and illustrating national character. But the author of 'Emma' confines herself chiefly to the middling classes of society; her most distinguished characters do not rise greatly above well-bred country gentlemen and ladies; and those which are sketched with most originality and precision, belong to a class below rather than above that standard. The narrative of all her novels is composed of such common occurrences as may have fallen under the observation of most folks; and her dramatis personæ conduct themselves upon the motives and principles which the readers may recognise as ruling their own, and that of most of their own acquaintances.

I may perhaps be allowed to supplement this by an extract from an article cited by Mr. Adams in his 'Chapters from Jane Austen'—an unexceptionable little book, save that in the Introduction he repeats his singular assertion that 'Evelina' is read now, if at all, from curiosity, and that 'Belinda' and 'Castle Rackrent' are read not at all. The article on British Novelists appeared in 'Fraser's Magazine' for January 1860 and was written by my father over his full initials 'W. F. P.,' which he frequently used in signing articles and letters.

Miss Austen is, of all his successors, the one who most

nearly resembles Richardson in the power ot impressing reality upon her characters. There is a perfection in the exhibition of Miss Austen's characters which no one else has approached ; and truth is never for an instant sacrificed in that delicate atmosphere of satire which pervades her works. . . .

. . . Miss Austen never attempts to describe a scene or a class of society with which she was not herself thoroughly acquainted. The conversations of ladies and gentlemen together are given, but no instance occurs of a scene in which men only are present.[1] [This is surely a noteworthy fact.] The uniform quality of her work is one most remarkable point to be observed in it. Let a volume be opened at any place; there is the same good English, the same refined style, the same simplicity and truth. . . . She has been accused of writing dull stories about ordinary people. But her supposed ordinary people are really not such very ordinary people. Let any one who is inclined to criticise on this score endeavour to construct from among the ordinary people of his own acquaintance one character that shall be capable of interesting any reader for ten minutes. It will then be found how great has been the discrimination of Miss Austen in the selection of her characters and how skilful is her treatment of them.

In both of these judgments is found one reason for the advantage in popularity of Miss Austen's work over that of her predecessors and contemporaries. It is, to put it baldly, this. It is in human

[1] There are two instances in the fragment, *The Watsons*, of very brief talk between two men alone. Also a 'peer of the realm' figures in *The Watsons*, which was not published in the days of the articles to which reference has been made.

nature that we like to see our own reflection, or what we fondly imagine to be our own reflection, to say nothing of that of our friends and neighbours. It is at once a gratification of harmless vanity and a satisfaction of a supposed or real sense of humour to be able to say, on reading a given passage, 'Just in this way should I (or would my friend So-and-so) have felt, spoken, and acted in the circumstances here depicted.' The feeling may be called the face of that medal of which the obverse is still to be seen, though the trick is by this time old enough, in the delight felt by many 'creatures sitting at a play' at the sight of a real hansom cab, a real man riding a real horse, or, to take it in its simplest form, Mr. Vincent Crummles's real pump and real tubs on the stage. Here is something that every spectator can apprehend at a glance, the while he congratulates himself on an apprehension just a little superior to that of his fellow-spectators. Each spectator, that is, thinks to himself 'Surely no one can take in the absolute truth of this quite so quickly as I do, since I well remember'—and then follows a crowd of trivial recollections. The process of thought is no doubt instantaneous and unconscious, but the approbation springs from an unrecognised sense of self-esteem. So in reading, the reader who is, or imagines that he is, 'above the average' takes a delight, which he would be sorry to explain to himself, in thinking that he sees just a little further and deeper than the first comer into fictitious motives, words, and actions, which he immediately recognises as being true to that part of human nature which is not unknown to himself. Herein lies the key to the puzzle of great temporary, or even permanent, success won by work which is but mediocre. Various instances of such successful work will surely arise to the recollection of readers, and it is therefore needless, as it would be discourteous, to cite any special example. Herein lies also part, but by no means all, of the secret of Miss Austen's continuing dominion. The reader who is 'above the average' does recognise in her characterisation and dialogue certain ideas which, as it seems to him, he himself might have embodied had circumstances favoured such an undertaking. 'Why, this is just what would happen—just what would be thought—just what would be said—I can see it all, understand it all myself. And since it is so easy to read, surely it would be easy enough to write if one had but the time and opportunity!' It is a not unpleasing self-delusion, and one that is not likely ever to be rooted out, since it combines two satisfactory attitudes of mind—a feeling of slight, not arrogant, superiority in appreciation to the general herd, and a virtuous joy and sincere admiration of a person just a little more capable than the admirer, and certainly more fortunate, in that chance gave her the time and occasion for so excellently expressing ideas and observations which are within that admirer's comprehension.

To be content with this as aught but the most

unimportant cause of what may be fairly called Miss Austen's supremacy would be to fulfil Dogberry's desire in one's own person and to write down Miss Austen as a novelist who had wit and talent enough to string together sensible and plausible commonplaces of everyday scenes and characters. That method has been of inestimable value to the kind of work to which allusion has been made, but there is infinitely more of course in Miss Austen's method and, one may surely add, in Miss Austen's inspiration. The words 'inspiration' and 'genius' are almost synonymous, and no true admirer of Miss Austen will for a moment admit that she was possessed of nothing more than a great and unique talent. Talent and close observation will do very much, but they will not avail to turn events and people which, as Madame de Staël had it, are *vulgaires*—that is to say, in their essence of a usual character—into types of enduring interest and charm, which, despite the rapid changes in habits and manners, delight the present, and one hopes the rising generation, just as much as they delighted Sir Walter Scott, to whom the ways and turns of speech of Miss Austen's folk were familiar as household words.

There is a passage in the article already quoted from 'Fraser' which touches this point closely:

> . . . There is never any deviation into the unnatural or exaggerated; and how worthy of all love and respect is the finely disciplined genius which rejects the forcible but transient modes of stimulating interest which can be so

easily employed when desired, and which knows how to trust to the never-failing principles of human nature! . . . It is true that the events are for the most part those of daily life, and the feelings are those connected with the usual joys and griefs of familiar existence; but these are the very events and feelings upon which the happiness or misery of most of us depends; and the field which embraces them, to the exclusion of the wonderful, the sentimental and the historical, is surely large enough, as it is certainly the one which admits of the most profitable cultivation. [With this, as to 'profitable cultivation,' I cannot, if I understand it aright, fully agree.] In the end, too, the novel of daily real life is that of which we are least apt to weary; a round of fancy balls would tire the most vigorous admirers of variety in costume, and the return to plain clothes would be hailed with greater delight than their occasional relinquishment ever gives. Miss Austen's personages are always in plain clothes, but no two suits are alike: all are worn with their appropriate differences, and under all human thoughts and feelings are at work.

This seems to me to indicate happily, though not specially so intended, the 'vast' which lies between the success of clever commonplace and the triumph of the genius which endues commonplace with rarity, which makes of characters that might be met any day in the present time, with a difference only of manners, forms of thought and emotion that may be encountered at any moment, a real possession for ever. Part of the secret of that magic which converted seemingly ordinary persons and events into matters of extraordinary delight and interest is touched on in the same article:

Her Contemporaries and Herself

> It is in the dramatic power with which her characters are exhibited that Miss Austen is unapproachable. Every one says the right thing in the right place and in the right way. The conservation of character is complete. We can never exactly predict what a particular person will say; there are no catch words or phrases perpetually recurring from the same person; yet we recognise as soon as spoken the truthful individuality of everything that is made to fall from each speaker. In this kind of genius she is without a rival, unless we look for one in the very highest name of our literature.

Words to the same effect were written by Macaulay; and if the comparison between Miss Austen and Shakspeare may to a first glance appear excessive, it will be found on closer inspection that, expressed as it is, it is in fact strictly within the limits of accurate criticism, or it might be more correct to say accurate appreciation of Miss Austen's greater qualities. My father continued:

> Sometimes in the admiration expressed for her greatest excellence, her claim to qualities exercised more in common with others has been overlooked; yet whenever accurate description is wanted, either of places or persons, it is supplied with ease and skill.

This remark was, it seems to me, well worth the making; for it certainly does appear that in Miss Austen's work, as indeed in all fiction that comes as near perfection as human skill can compass in its own line, the seemingly lesser merits are apt to be altogether overshadowed by the evidences of genius found in characterisation and in dialogue. Yet surely it is precisely these seeming lesser merits, this close attention and industry in the consideration and treatment of the smallest detail, that help to make the work so excellent as it is. There is, be it observed, no Balzac-like overloading of detail (which of us has not sometimes quailed before the merciless description of every button on every gaiter in the opening of a Balzac novel?), no confusing of the general effect aimed at by divagations into byways of a too minute portraiture of places and persons. All is in harmony with, and subdued to, the central design. And yet in all the novels there has been detected only one slip, to be presently mentioned, in the finest details of description. Here then we have good general reason for the fact that Miss Austen retains, and I believe will always retain, her hold as a great novelist upon all readers who care for literature, while other writers whose genius was of a high order are comparatively forgotten. There are passages, isolated passages, more brilliant perhaps in actual wit than anything of Miss Austen's to be found in these writers, there are scenes more daring and more dramatic, but she stands alone in that Shakspearian gift and practice of being always absolutely true to nature, to the nature of each and every personage of her creation, clever or stupid, agreeable or disagreeable. Shakspearian too is the art which makes the disagreeable people and the fools very entertaining company. Add to these qualities that seemingly easy truth of detail and that perfect charm of style to which reference has been made, and you have surely a unique combination. This much granted, it may be not uninteresting to look into certain points of contact, of difference, and of contact with a difference, between Miss Austen and the other noted writers of and before her date.

CHAPTER IV

REFERRING back to Sir Walter Scott's article in the 'Quarterly Review,' I do not well or fully understand this passage :

> The author of 'Emma' confines herself to the middling classes of society ; her most distinguished characters do not rise greatly above well-bred country gentlemen and ladies ; and those which are sketched with most originality and precision, belong to a class below rather than above that standard.

The first phrase of the sentence is undoubtedly accurate, and the same point is noted in the 'Fraser' article : 'Hardly ever is a person of greater rank than a baronet introduced, nor [this is not in complete accordance with Sir Walter Scott's concluding phrase] does any fall below the professional and commercial classes.' I do not identify the personages whom Sir Walter Scott had in his mind when he wrote that the characters sketched with most originality and precision belonged to a class rather below than above well-bred country society. To take a few instances, the immortal Miss Bates in 'Emma' would not, to be sure, have been ranked among 'county people,' but that was an accident of means, not of manners, nor yet, it may be said, of birth, since she was the daughter of a former Vicar of Highbury, who had left her widowed mother and herself in very straitened circumstances. Mr. Martin, the young farmer in the same novel, though absolutely true to life and consistent, like all Miss Austen's characters, is not of sufficient importance to be cited in support of Sir Walter Scott's dictum; nor is Harriet Smith, the foolish nobody with whom Mr. Martin was in love; while Mrs. Goddard the schoolmistress, and other characters below her in social position, lifelike as they are, do but pass rapidly from time to time across the scene. Again, in 'Northanger Abbey,' which shared with 'Emma' the place of favourite with Sir Walter Scott, the Thorpes, to be sure, are the essence of vulgarity, but yet by mere position they hardly answer to the great novelist's description. And in 'Mansfield Park,' to take one other instance, Lieutenant Price and his wife, sunk with marriage by him, are the only persons of importance who could not be 'passed' into the county society of which Sir Thomas Bertram was a prominent member. The matter would seem to lie rather thus—that while Miss Burney, Miss Edgeworth, and Miss Ferrier dealt at will, and with a perfectly equal hand as to praise and blame, like and dislike, with characters of the aristocratic, the middle, and the lower class, Miss Austen never went much above or (*pace* Sir Walter Scott) much below the middle class, a term which was in her days less elastic than it now has become. Hence, no doubt to some extent, the almost absolute perfection of her work. The world of fashion was not to her taste, probably, and it did not naturally come in her way to mix in it. Her knowledge of the lower classes was no doubt confined to villagers, of whom here and there in the novels we get glimpses, but no more than glimpses, such as the excellent glimpse of the carpenter in 'Mansfield Park.' She never went into those questions of political-fashionable life which are prominent in Miss Edgeworth's 'Patronage' and which are more or less touched on in others of Miss Edgeworth's novels.

She never attempted the tragic line taken with great success by Miss Burney when she describes Harrel's death in 'Cecilia,' nor did she ever attempt to depict the course of reckless dissipation which led to that death, or the not dissimilar courses which are shown in many of Miss Edgeworth's shorter stories, notably in 'The Lottery Ticket.' Nor did she ever adventure such a description of an ignorant gardener's domestic life as is given by Miss Edgeworth in 'Forester.' Least of all did she try, as Miss Ferrier did, to draw a character of which she could not by any possibility have any first-hand knowledge. This was Miss Ferrier's case in 'The Inheritance.' Perhaps never was a more hopelessly unnatural character drawn by a novelist not devoid of genius than Lewiston, the scoundrel, Americanised as he is supposed to be, in the novel just named. Lewiston is like nothing that has ever been seen upon this earth. Miss Ferrier's idea was to make him coarse, vulgar, a blackmailing impostor, and American. She had no knowledge on which to found her conception, and the hand which in the same novel drew so excellent a portrait of the essentially common Black family, redeemed by the really good qualities of the lifelike Adam Black, common himself only from narrowness and lack of education, presented us with a very monster of fiction in Lewiston. It is but to be supposed that Miss Ferrier took all Americans below the aristocratic class to be persons *feræ naturæ*, and proceeded to draw upon her imagination for the vulgarest things that the vulgarest man in the world could conceive and act upon. Therefore, acquainted with English as well as Scots manners of fashion, and equally well acquainted with the manners of the Scots peasantry and of the then Scots 'ministers,' Miss Ferrier, drawing upon a bank of imagination where there was no account of information, made her 'American,' as she frequently calls him, deliver such a speech as this, which he makes when, thinking himself secure in his disgraceful fraud, he has, by preying upon Mrs. St. Clair's terror, established himself as a guest to be cajoled in every way in Miss St. Clair's house. He is dissatisfied with the best efforts of the head cook in dainty dishes, and exclaims:

What do you think, for instance, of a fine, jolly, juicy, thirty-pound round of well-corned beef and parsnips? or a handsome leg of pork and pease-pudding, and a couple of fat geese well stuffed with sage and onions, swimming in apple-sauce? Ah! these are the dishes for me!' and he rubbed his hands with horrid glee.

Now this is very far from being an unfair or exaggerated instance of the ludicrously and unpleasantly impossible fashion in which the character of Lewiston is imagined and drawn throughout. And yet he occurs in the same book with the inimitable Miss Pratt and Lord Rossville, who are equal and like to some of Miss Austen's characters in that, intolerable bores in their different ways, they are yet a source of never-failing delight to readers.

We may be very sure that if Miss Austen had introduced an American into any of her novels the character would have been studied from life, though not as a portrait of any one individual. She may probably never have come across any Americans: she certainly would not have played, as Miss Ferrier has done, the fabled German philosopher's camel-trick. Here is one point of superiority both to Miss Ferrier and to Miss Burney. There are absolutely no monsters of impossibility or even any characters of improbability, from Sir Thomas Bertram down to Knightley's bailiff, a person whom we know well, although we never actually meet him, in all the novels. Miss Burney errs but comparatively seldom in this regard. Yet it must be admitted that Lionel Tyrold in 'Camilla' is fully as improbable a character, though the improbability is not so obviously extravagant as is Miss Ferrier's Lewiston. The intention clearly was to give an illustration of 'Video meliora proboque, deteriora sequor.' But the changes from virtuous resolve or repentance to the most selfish and reckless wickedness are so abrupt and so coarsely handled—an unusual defect in Miss Burney—that the effect is that of a glaring daub rather than of a finished picture. Miss Austen's own favourite, Mr. Dubster, in the same novel may be set against the oddly blundered Lionel as a good example of a caricature in which the colours are laid on 'with a good fat brush' broadly, but not too broadly for reasonable merriment. Again, while in 'Evelina' there is no character that one rejects as impossible (where Miss Burney got her inspiration of the Branghtons is a marvel), yet there are things which in the old sense of the word shock the understanding. With all the odd manners of the time, one cannot but wonder how Captain Mirvan and Madame Duval were tolerated by the society in the midst of which we find them, though this, to be sure, is easily forgotten in the rattling comedy of the scenes wherein they appear.

In 'Cecilia' there is certainly one character which appears out of drawing in itself and out of harmony with the rest by reason of its extravagance. This is—to leave aside the Solomon-Eagle-like Albany—Briggs, the miser, who is, most improbably, one of Cecilia's guardians. But of the gross caricature effect of this personage there is a very simple explanation in the fact which we learn from Miss Annie Raine Ellis's excellent preface, that Miss Burney, lacking Dickens's keenness to see that the actual must be altered in novel-writing, just as the stage-focus must be humoured in play-writing, drew the character of

Briggs straight from Nollekens the sculptor, 'trait for trait,' as it is put by Miss Ellis, who adds that

> Briggs is no caricature of Nollekens, but to take a miser, barely English, the son of an Antwerp miser, and make him out to be 'a warm man' in the City of London, was enough to make readers in 1782 consider Briggs a caricature, and to leave in the mind of a reader in 1882 a strong sense of unfitness which is explained if we believe Briggs to have been lifted out of one set of circumstances and pushed into another set, to suit the plan of this novel.

There is another marked difference, greatly to Miss Austen's advantage, between her method and Miss Burney's. Miss Austen's English and style were, with the exception of a few slips in grammar, such as 'those sort of things,' impeccable, but never pedantic. As Mr. Austin Dobson writes:

> Going over her pages, pencil in hand, the antiquarian annotator is struck by their excessive 'modernity,' and, after a prolonged examination, discovers, in this century-old record, nothing more fitted for the exercise of his ingenuity than such an obsolete game at cards as 'cassino' [cassino is not so very obsolete] or 'quadrille.' The philologist is in no better case. He speedily arrives at the conclusion that he will find in Madame D'Arblay and Miss Edgeworth—to cite writers who are more or less in Miss Austen's line—a far more profitable hunting-ground for archaisms, and he probably falls back upon admiration of the finished and perspicuous style.

It is precisely this finished and perspicuous style that we miss in Madame D'Arblay of the Diary and Miss Burney of the novels. In 'Cecilia,' as

Miss Ellis says, 'homely or odd expressions are left straggling (probably from haste) among patches of stately Johnsonese.' [It is quite certain, by the way, from the Doctor's own assurance, that Johnson had no hand in 'Cecilia.'] *Stroam*, a corruption of *stroll*, used also by Miss Edgeworth, is constantly employed, and Miss Burney frequently coined words, quoting Dr. Johnson as an excuse, but forgetting that when the Doctor made words he made them according to philological rules, of which she was ignorant. It may be confidently asserted that not an expression, not a word, to which a philologist can take exception is to be found in all Miss Austen's novels.

In taking leave of 'Cecilia' for the present it may be worth while to call attention to an odd coincidence which of course has not escaped previous notice. In the last chapter of 'Cecilia' occurs this passage: '"The whole of this unfortunate business," said Dr. Lyster, "has been the result of PRIDE AND PREJUDICE"' (in very large capitals), and the phrase is twice afterwards repeated in the same large capitals which distinguish the word HEIRESS in the last few lines of the novel. I have a kind of recollection that the question whether this passage was or was not consciously or unconsciously present to Miss Austen's mind when she gave a title to the story of Elizabeth Bennet and Darcy has been worked out by a previous writer, but I have tried in vain to verify it. Miss Ellis however, generally a most trustworthy authority, states simply, in a footnote to her preface to 'Evelina,' that 'Miss Austen took from the last sentence of " Camilla " [it is not the last sentence] the name of her novel " Pride and Prejudice."' Miss Austen's enthusiasm for 'Camilla' may have been partly due to her having been a subscriber to the book when it came out in 1796—her name stands between those of 'George Aust, Esq.,' and 'Mrs. Ayton'—but chiefly of course to a generous admiration for anything that Miss Burney might write.

CHAPTER V

IN Miss Edgeworth there are not such glaring defects as can be found in Miss Burney and Miss Ferrier. Some of her characters seem now extravagant—as, for instance, King Corny in 'Ormonde'—and give the impression of being taken straight from life, a piece of too direct portraiture. But then these characters are never in any way 'out of the picture,' as is Briggs in 'Cecilia.' Miss Edgeworth's genius, however, if it was frequently employed on both higher and lower ranks of society than those with which Miss Austen dealt, was certainly less tempered and polished 'to the very finger-nail' than was Miss Austen's. To be sure she differed from Miss Burney in her usually remarkable accuracy of style and statement, but this accuracy sometimes came near the confines of pedantry. The love of accuracy is shown in the lists of *errata* appended to her first edition, while the tendency to pedantry can be traced in the footnotes *passim*. She certainly had a remarkable scope. It was her knowledge and treatment of Irish scenes and characters that particularly commanded Sir Walter Scott's admiration and, as we have seen, spurred him on to do as he said for Scotland what she had done for Ireland in fiction. But she was equally successful in her observation and representation of English life and character, and, like a much later novelist—Charles Lever—she could reproduce some kinds of Scots character and diction as naturally and correctly as she did those Irish traits, in delineation of which nobody of the time approached her. In all she wrote a fine eye for character can be detected; but we cannot hold it as fine as Miss Austen's, since not very infrequently we find the black and white laid on with too little care for the nice shades of tone which Miss Austen never neglected. The good people are sometimes unco guid, and are for that reason perilously like bores. Mr. Percy, for instance, in 'Patronage' is a person of doubtless excellence, but would any one suffer his company so gladly as that of Mr. Knightley in 'Emma,' who was, from all we know of him, as excellent a man as one could wish to meet? But then he was not, like Mr. Percy, a kind of statue of perfection. He possessed a touch or two of human frailty in temper and in jealousy, and is undoubtedly the more interesting for them. Then, contrast Caroline Percy in the same novel of Miss Edgeworth's with Jane Bennet in 'Pride and Prejudice.' In each case the intention seems to have been to represent a girl of a natural equable temperament cultivated to the utmost extent by the discipline of self-control. But what a difference in the treatment! Jane Bennet may seem touched with prudery to the now rising generation. They can hardly be expected to realise with any vividness the manners of a time when a sort of perfume of Grandisonian stateliness still haunted the air, and when 'nerves' were almost unknown save as a fashionable affectation. Still, a young woman or a young man of the present day would, one fancies, be quick enough to distinguish between the artifice which cannot hide itself in the drawing of Caroline Percy—who, to be sure, is but a well-meaning prig (and Mary Douglas in Miss Ferrier's 'Marriage' is but little more)—and the nature which one recognises and esteems in Jane Bennet, though perhaps it may seem strange enough, and therefore no doubt all the truer to nature, that any one should fall in love with her when her sister Elizabeth was present. But Bingley, of course, being in many ways opposite in disposition to Jane as Darcy was to Eliza, was the very man to fall in love with Jane.

As for Miss Edgeworth's general method and style as compared with Miss Austen's, if the words, which would not be altogether inappropriate, 'a full flowing roundness inclining to length,' were applied to her novels, there might perhaps be an inclination to lay some stress on the last word. Most of the novels ('Helen' may be cited as a notable exception) are indeed somewhat lengthy as opposed to *long*, and that apart from the touch of preachiness which is more or less common to her, to Miss Burney, and to Miss Ferrier. In Miss Burney's first and on the whole best work, 'Evelina,' this peculiarity may be observed chiefly in the letters which pass between Evelina and Mr. Villars. The very first lines of the book will serve as an example. They are the beginning of a letter from Evelina to Mr. Villars: 'Can any thing, my good sir, be more painful to a friendly mind, than a necessity of communicating disagreeable intelligence? Indeed, it is sometimes difficult to determine whether the relater or the receiver of evil tidings is most to be pitied.' This kind of thing, however, belonged to the time in which Miss Burney wrote, and therefore must not be counted an actual fault in her, though the fact that there is nothing like it in Miss Austen is one of the reasons for the superiority of Miss Austen both in excellence and in popularity. In Miss Ferrier the trait comes out a good deal in the dialogue, which not the less is on occasions both witty and humorous. Opening 'Destiny' at random, I light upon an instance:

> 'My dear Ronald [said Captain Malcolm to his son], I was in hopes your good sense would, before now, have suggested to you what a dangerous habit you are acquiring of constantly wishing.'
>
> 'Dangerous, papa!' repeated Ronald, 'how can that possibly be?'
>
> 'I consider it very dangerous,' replied the father mildly; 'and so will you, I am very sure, when you come to reflect upon it. It is positive waste of time and thought and contentment. Wishing has been called the hectic of a fool. If it is not the proof of a dissatisfied mind (which, in your case, I trust it is not) it inevitably leads to it; for wishing is not

very far from murmuring. It is not to inculcate an improvident habit, but a contented mind, that we are charged to take no thought of to-morrow.'

And in this way the dialogue, or broken monologue, goes on for more than another page.

So does it happen also with Miss Edgeworth. Take an extract from a dialogue between Mr. and Mrs. Percy and their son Godfrey, whom one knew in one's childhood as the brother of Rosamond, heroine of 'The Purple Jar,' a story in which Mrs. Percy—the family name is, I think, given for the first time in 'Patronage'—figures in a singularly unamiable fashion. Rosamond also appears in 'Patronage,' but her part in this particular dialogue need not be quoted. She and Godfrey are certainly the most human members of the Percy family. The talk is of a certain Miss Hauton who has captivated Godfrey's passing affection, and who is the daughter of a woman of dubious reputation.

> 'Undoubtedly,' said Mr. Percy, 'exceptions must not merely be allowed, but will force themselves in favor of superior merit, of extraordinary excellence, which will rise above every unfavorable [1] circumstance in any class, in any condition of life in which it may exist, which will throw off any stigma, however disgraceful, counteract all prepossession, however potent, rise against all power of expression, redeem a family, redeem a race.'

[1] It will be observed from the spelling here that the American omission of the *u* in such words as *favour* has at least decent warrant, and indeed many so-called Americanisms are readily traced to good English expressions of a past time. 'I reckon,' for instance, is still perfectly extant in the West Country.

To borrow an illustration from the stage, one can imagine that such a speech as this, attributed to a magnanimous father and delivered intelligently and intelligibly by a well-trained actor of a school now all but extinct, might have gained genuine applause from an audience who expected the height of fine sentiment. Nowadays it seems, in the pages of a novel, not only didactic but of the stage, stagey, which is a very different thing from dramatic. And, as was pointed out by Lord Macaulay and by subsequent writers, Miss Austen, though in her grown-up time she never put anything in dramatic form, possessed the real dramatic faculty to an extraordinary degree. Miss Edgeworth did try the dramatic form. 'Old Poz,' a bright simple little sketch, in its plot identical with 'The Maid and the Magpie,' is still occasionally acted in young folks' theatricals and is fit enough for the purpose. 'Eton Montem' is also cast in dramatic form, and is an odd instance at once of Miss Edgeworth's accuracy and inaccuracy. It is clear that the author took every pains to become acquainted with all the details of ceremony and costume observed in that long defunct entertainment, although from 'Eton of Old, or Eighty Years Since' (London: Griffith, Farran, & Co., 1892) one would certainly infer that a contest by election for the captainship was, even in the exceptional circumstances described by Miss Edgeworth, an unknown thing, and that the captainship invariably went to a Colleger. However that may be, Miss Edgeworth, just as Miss Ferrier did in the case of

Lewiston the 'American,' certainly evolved Eton boys, their ways, manners, and talk, from her own inner consciousness. No Eton boys ever behaved like that, as one may imagine that no Westminster boys ever behaved as do the Westminster boys in an otherwise characteristically good short story, 'The Good Aunt.' The truth is that Miss Edgeworth did not fully understand boys and their ways. That Miss Austen did is evident enough from several passages in 'Mansfield Park,' just as it is clear from the Fairbairn scene in 'The Inheritance' that Miss Ferrier was well acquainted with the disagreeable side of a family life wherein the children tyrannise a household. Another of Miss Edgeworth's shorter efforts, 'The Knapsack,' is cast in a dramatic mould. It contains a dramatic situation and some pretty, old-fashioned songs, but is, in the proper sense of the word, hopelessly undramatic.[1] Now it seems certain that if Miss Austen had thought fit to give a setting in theatrical form to any of her conceptions the result would have been a thing not perhaps fitted as it stood for the stage, but surely in its essence *dramatic.* This may be a fit place to quote in full that opinion expressed by Lord Macaulay to which reference has before been made. It was put forth in an article in the 'Edinburgh Review' for January 1843.

[1] It may be noted that in the second scene of this little play is another instance of an 'Americanism' coming from a good English source. The 'Serjeant' says of his men, 'I've seen them march quite another guess sort of way.'

Jane Austen

Shakespeare has had neither equal nor second. But among the writers who . . . have approached nearest to the manner of the great master, we have no hesitation in placing Jane Austen, a woman of whom England is justly proud. She has given us a multitude of characters, all in a certain sense commonplace, all such as we meet every day. Yet they are all as perfectly discriminated from each other as if they were the most eccentric of human beings. There are, for instance, four clergymen, none of whom we should be surprised to find in any parsonage in the kingdom—Mr. Edward Ferrars, Mr. Henry Tilney, Mr. Edmund Bertram, and Mr. Elton. They are all specimens of the upper part of the middle class. They have all been liberally educated. They all lie under the restraints of the same sacred profession. They are all young. They are all in love. Not one of them has any hobby horse, to use the phrase of Sterne. Not one has a ruling passion, such as we read of in Pope. Who would not have expected them to be insipid likenesses of each other? No such thing. Harpagon is not more unlike to Jourdain, Joseph Surface is not more unlike to Sir Lucius O'Trigger, than every one of Miss Austen's young divines to all his reverend brethren. And all this is done by touches so delicate that they elude analysis, that they defy the powers of description, and that we know them to exist only by the general effect to which they have contributed.

Never surely was a more perspicuous, a more enthusiastic, and, what is more to the present purpose, a juster estimate of one great writer delivered by another, who, as we have seen, was very far from lacking in enthusiasm for the work of Miss Burney, for whom he took up his trenchant steel against Croker's somewhat clumsy bludgeon. But he could not, with the justice which distinguishes the passage just quoted, have compared Miss Burney directly or indirectly to Shakspeare or Molière. The great dramatic instinct always more or less present in Miss Austen was wanting there. Yet, as might be guessed from Miss Austen's unstinted admiration for Miss Burney, and especially for that work of Miss Burney's which is not ranked highest (her admiration for 'Camilla' seems, from a passage in 'Belinda,' to have been shared by Miss Edgeworth), the younger did owe something to the elder author.

I have allowed myself to quote freely from Miss Annie Raine Ellis, and it seems to me that she has touched this matter finely and tersely in the concluding paragraph of her preface to 'Cecilia:'

> It is scarcely possible to read some of Miss Edgeworth's early writings, and quite impossible to read the first three novels of Miss Austen, without perceiving how much both writers were affected by what Miss Burney had written. It is shown even more by what they avoid in her than by what they imitate. They have absorbed all that is best in her books, and with humour beyond her own, they make those of their heroines who are most after their own hearts act as Evelina, Cecilia, or Camilla, never could or would have done. This is more specially said of Miss Austen. Miss Edgeworth was reared among the ministers of the new cult of Utility, and might perhaps have made her Belindas and Carolines prudent to as painful an excess, if she had never read 'Cecilia,' but should we have had Elinor Dashwood, and Elizabeth Bennet? Such a first book as 'Pride and Prejudice' written at one-and-twenty, is more wonderful than all that Frances Burney ever wrote. Yet if she never

> reaches Miss Austen's surety of touch and harmony of tone, she may be said to aim higher. Miss Austen always works within limits, of her own choice ; imposed upon her, it may be, by her own judgment, which told her to write comedy. There is not one death in her six novels, and very few disasters. Frances Burney chose larger canvases, some subjects more tragic, and some models more heroic in their proportions. She moved to tears three generations : one which was growing old while she was young, one whose life ran with her own, and one born while she was famous. She just missed knowing Richardson ; she was sought and honoured by Scott.

This, as the conclusion of a well-judged panegyric on Miss Burney, strikes me as unusually and capitally discriminating criticism, and it is certainly truer of Miss Austen than of Miss Edgeworth that by an admiring study of Miss Burney she learnt even more what to avoid than what to imitate.

Her Contemporaries and Herself

CHAPTER VI

IT might not be difficult to find many points of contact, with a difference, between Miss Austen and the three writers whose work we have been considering in comparison with hers. But it would certainly be lengthy, and one or two instances may suffice, one particularly in which all four authors meet on common ground. In the first place it may be worth noting that in 'Belinda' Miss Edgeworth more than once touches, but only touches, on the line taken by Miss Austen in 'Northanger Abbey.' Thus in vol. i. of 'Belinda' we find a sly hit at Mrs. Radcliffe, when Dr. X—— (the pseudonym given, it would seem, to Dr. Moore, author of 'Zeluco,' throughout the novels) says to Belinda :

My dear Miss Portman, you will put a stop to a number of charming stories by this prudence of yours—a romance called the Mysterious Boudoir, of nine volumes at least, might be written on this subject, if you would only condescend to act like almost all other heroines, that is to say, without common sense.

In the second volume of the same novel Mr. Percival has this speech :

You know it is a ruled case, in all romances, that, when

a lover and his mistress go out riding together, some adventure must befal them. The horse must run away with the lady, and the gentleman must catch her in his arms just as her neck is about to be broken. If the horse has been too well trained for the heroine's purpose, 'some footpad, bandit fierce, or mountaineer,' some jealous rival must make his appearance quite unexpectedly at the turn of a road, and the lady must be carried off—robes flying—hair streaming—like Buerger's Leonora. Then her lover must come to her rescue just in the proper moment. But if the damsel cannot conveniently be run away with, she must, as the last resource, tumble into a river to make herself interesting, and the hero must be at least half drowned in dragging her out, that she may be under eternal obligations to him, and at last be forced to marry him out of pure gratitude.

These, as has been said, are but touches, and do but show that a reaction against the Mrs. Radcliffe method was 'in the air' before the time of 'Northanger Abbey.' There is certainly no reason for imagining that these passages, or others like them which could probably be hunted up in other books of the time, had any real connection with 'Northanger Abbey.' Just as we may feel sure that Miss Austen would never have set to work on a book of the same kind as 'Belinda,' so may we be confident that Miss Edgeworth never could have compassed the 'surety of touch and harmony of tone' found in 'Northanger Abbey,' truly an exquisite book, and, so far as I know, the only one of Miss Austen's in which the author deliberately makes mock at her own characters, appearing as it were as a kind of satirical chorus to the personages that she has put on her stage. Of this there may be more to say later.

The ground to which reference has been made on which all four authors meet is that of 'theatricals,' almost as popular in those days as now. There is but little on this topic in Miss Burney and Miss Ferrier, while in Miss Edgeworth's 'Patronage' and in Miss Austen's 'Mansfield Park' there are capital scenes afforded by the subject. Excerpts from what has been written by each author on an identical theme give however a convenient opportunity of comparing the different styles. One may note by the way that in Miss Burney and Miss Ferrier we hear of masquerades and of the odd entertainment—analogous to the modern 'Drawing-Room Tea'—known as 'seeing masks;' while in Miss Burney one often finds 'tickets' as the equivalent for visiting-cards. This use, as my brother Sir Frederick Pollock reminds me, still survives in the language used by and to Indian native servants.[1]

The only touch of private theatricals in Miss Burney's novels occurs in 'Camilla' (vol. ii. p. 248 of the first edition). It is a very primitive piece of business, but sufficiently shows that amateur acting was a recognised social amusement of the day. The

[1] Here is an instance: 'Mem-Sahib ko hamára tikat do'—'Give our [honorific plural for *my*] card to your mistress.'

incident takes place at Mrs. Arlbery's country house, where

> Lionel, ever restless, seized the opportunity to patrol the attic regions of the house, when, meeting with a capacious lumber room, he returned to assure the whole party it would make an admirable theatre, and to ask who would come forth to spout with him.
>
> Mr. Macderfey said, he did not know one word of any part, but he could never refuse anything that might contribute to the company's pleasure.
>
> Away they sped together, and in a few minutes reversed the face of everything. Old sofas, bedsteads, and trunks, large family chests, deal boxes and hampers, carpets and curtains rolled up for summer, tables with two legs, and chairs without bottoms, were truckled [here is one of Miss Burney's coined words, *truckle* n.s. being 'a small wheel or castor'] from the middle to one end of the room, and arranged to form a semi-circle, with seats in front, to form a pit. Carpets were then uncovered and untied, to be spread for the stage, and curtains, with as little mercy, were unfurled, and hung up to make a scene.

There follows a dull farcical incident—which, like the whole of the episode, shows the author by no means at her best—of a suspected booby-trap, arising out of the arrangements made for the improvised stage; and then we read how

> the ensign, in mock heroics, solemnly prostrated himself to Miss Dennel, pouring into her delighted ears, from various shreds and scraps of different tragedies, the most high-flown and egregiously ill-adapted compliments : while the Major,

less absurdly, though scarce less passionately, made Camilla his Juliet, and whispered the tenderest lines of Romeo.

In 'Evelina' there is a brief but eloquent description of Garrick, as Ranger in Hoadley's comedy 'The Suspicious Husband,' and an excellent scene in the boxes of the playhouse in which Mr. Lovel and Captain Mirvan are the chief figures; and in 'Cecilia' there is a scene at an opera-rehearsal, passing partly in the boxes and partly behind the scenes when the rehearsal is over; but there is no description of what 'behind the scenes' was like in those days, such as Miss Austen would surely have given had it been in her way to deal with such a business. In 'Camilla,' again, we have a passage concerning a troop of disgracefully incompetent strolling players who did enact 'Othello' at what is now, or lately was, known as 'a fit-up'—at 'the town of Etherington.' There is again here more of rough farce than of high comedy, and the only real interest lies in the facts shown that Miss Burney was well acquainted with theatrical matters, and that the cockney inversion of *v* and *w*—on Dickens's correct use of which ('Spell it with a *we*, Sammy, spell it with a *we*!') doubt is sometimes still cast—was fully recognised in Miss Burney's time. Part of 'the humour of it' is that every performer save one speaks with a very marked dialect. Cassio comes from Norfolk, Desdemona from Worcestershire, Brabantio from Somersetshire.

Othello himself proved a true Londoner; and with his

famed soldier-like eloquence in the Senate-scene, thus began his celebrated defence :

> Most potent, grave, and rewerend Seignors,
> My wery noble and approwed good masters,
> . . . I vill a round unwarnish'd tale deliver.'

And so on. The exaggeration is obvious, but must have been founded on a known London dialect. In Miss Ferrier's 'Destiny' we come upon the time when French plays were the rage for amateur acting. Although it was Madame de Feuillade—Mr. Austen's niece, whose husband was guillotined in the French Revolution—who introduced theatricals at Steventon, there is nothing to show that they acted French plays, though it seems probable. In 'Destiny,' then, we find Lady Elizabeth Glenroy—who had in her day, then very long past, been a beauty, and who still considers herself both a beauty and a star of fashion—informing her stepdaughter Edith that Florinda, Lady Waldegrave, Lady Elizabeth's daughter by a former marriage, is about to have a French play and ballet performed by amateurs at her house in London. Miss Ferrier's treatment of the matter well illustrates the terse and clear description of her method given in the Prefatory Note by the late George Bentley—a fine and well-equipped critic—to his standard edition of her novels :

> The almost exceptional position [he wrote] which they occupy as satirising the foibles rather than the serious faults of human nature, and the caustic character of that satire, mingled with such bright wit and genial humour, give Miss Ferrier a place to herself in English fiction.

Now in Miss Austen, and it is one of her superior charms, there is nothing one would justly call *caustic*; and it is therefore not for comparison in the strict sense, but to illustrate one reason why Miss Austen's method is justly preferred, that recurrence is made to Miss Ferrier.

Lady Elizabeth, resembling Dickens's Mrs. Skewton in that, a mere wreck, she imagines herself still beautiful and fascinating, observes to Edith:

'It is particularly fortunate that I should have regained my looks at this time, as I have a little plan in contemplation, the success of which will depend very materially upon my appearance. You are aware, I suppose, of Florinda's intention of having a French play and ballet performed here next week. I should have been happy to take a part in the play; but really the labour of getting by heart I found would be too much for me; in fact I cannot take the trouble to commit anything to memory; then the fatigue of dancing in the ballet is more than I am yet able for; indeed, the very thoughts of it made Florinda, poor dear, quite wretched—so I gave that up also; but something is expected of me on the occasion.'

'Nothing more, I am sure,' said Edith, 'than that you should be a pleased spectator.'

'You are quite mistaken,' said her Ladyship, with an air of displeasure; 'anybody may be that, but *I* must be something more; I am expected to show off; it is the tax always levied on talented persons; in fact we are public property.' Edith saw remonstrance would be vain, so she remained silent. 'However, as I cannot undertake the drudgery of the play, and am not equal to the exertion required in the ballet, I have devised a little interlude for myself, which I think will have a charming effect. I intend to come upon the stage in a little car as a—a—in short, as Venus, with little Dudley in my lap, as Cupid, in a flesh-coloured silk dress and silver wings. My own dress I have not determined upon; but I think of having it *couleur de soupir étouffé*; that, you know, will be appropriate, and I shall sing "Ecco d' Amor il Tempio." The design is pretty—don't you think so?'

Edith felt as if she could both laugh and cry at the idea of this preposterous exhibition, and she said something about Lady Waldegrave not approving of it.

'Oh, as to that, the whole is to be kept a profound secret from Florinda, and to be quite a charming surprise to her. You must therefore promise me not to breathe a syllable of it to anybody; indeed, had I not entertained a very high opinion of your prudence and good taste, I should not have let you into my secret.'

Edith would fain have tried to open the infatuated old woman's eyes to the folly and degradation of making herself a spectacle for the finger of scorn to point at; but her gentle remonstrances were like the sweet south blowing, not on a bank of violets, but of nettles. [The use of south for south wind is curious.] Lady Elizabeth cut them short with much asperity.

There is more in the same strain concerning an idea which, luckily for Lady Elizabeth and for Lady Waldegrave and for everybody else save scandal-lovers, never took shape; but enough has been quoted to mark the difference between Miss Ferrier's and Miss Austen's habits and methods of seeing and representing things as they go. It is not likely that Miss Austen would have chosen or cared to dwell on such a picture as that of an old woman bent on the hopeless adventure of seeming still young, charming, and a leader of fashion, undertaking in secret from her daughter a performance which she well knew would shock that daughter's sense of fashionable (if nought else) propriety. Had such a picture been necessary to any scheme of hers, we may be very sure that it would have been handled with a less caustic and certainly not less amusing touch. There would have been no such phrases as 'infatuated old woman,' 'folly and degradation,' 'spectacle for the finger of scorn to point at.' All would have been 'used gently;' we should have had the moral effect of the scene, and yet have retained a sense of amusement the bitterness of which was but a sub-acid. Miss Ferrier's way of treating it is her own, and is certainly strong enough; but one imagines that Miss Austen, with equal strength, would have left a less unpleasing impression.

Miss Edgeworth's way of dealing with her characters after they have got themselves into the jealous web of amateur acting, comes considerably nearer to Miss Austen's; and therefore the points of difference between the two writers on this matter are all the more worth noting. Lovers of Miss Austen are of course well up in the perfectly touched scenes which take place during the rehearsals for the projected play in 'Mansfield Park,' and wili equally of course forgive me for making extracts from them as well as from Miss Edgeworth's analogous scenes in 'Patronage.'

CHAPTER VII

THE people who plunge, greatly daring, into amateur acting in Miss Edgeworth's 'Patronage' are the Falconer family, and more than one of them is both knave and fool, an unpleasing combination which it may be fairly said is not encountered once in Miss Austen's novels. The preliminary arrangements for the play—Hill's English version of Voltaire's 'Zaïre'—serve as a cloak for a great deal of mean manœuvring in other directions on the part of Mrs. Falconer, and are furthermore employed to accentuate the more and the most disagreeable qualities of Mrs. Falconer's daughters, so as to bring into high relief the entirely amiable disposition of the heroine, Caroline, who, as has been earlier said, is apt to annoy a reader by unco guidness. Such an artifice was not in Miss Austen's line, or at least not, as we shall presently see, so transparent an artifice; but for the present let us note the fact that here, as elsewhere, Miss Edgeworth's disagreeable people, drawn certainly to the life, are almost as disagreeable to read about as they would be to meet, while Miss Austen's cross-grained folk have always for the reader that penetrating sense of 'amusement' which makes them entertaining instead of annoying. It may have been a conscious or half-conscious sense of having dwelt with too disagreeable an iteration on petty traits of manners and character—among them the curious fashion of the time according to which ladies were in the habit of selling cast-off dresses to their lady's-maids and driving hard bargains for them—that made Miss Edgeworth sum up matters thus :

> In due time, consequently, the Turkish dresses were in great forwardness.—Lest we should never get to the play, we forbear to relate all the various frettings, jealousies, clashing vanities, and petty quarrels, which occurred between the actresses and their friends, during the getting up of this piece and its rehearsals. We need mention only that the seeds of irreconcilable dislike were sown at this time between the Miss Falconers and their dear friends the Lady Arlingtons. There was some difficulty made by Lady Anne about lending her diamond crescent for Zara's turban ; Miss Georgiana could never forgive this. And Lady Frances, on her part, was provoked beyond measure by an order from the Duke, her uncle, forbidding her to appear on the stage.

The whole description of the preparations is lifelike, but inclines a little to tedium by excess now of *mere* lifelikeness, now of a tendency to caricature. When we come to the actual performance there are many touches of Miss Edgeworth's fine perception, and we come also upon a curious point of difference between Miss Austen's method and hers.

There is true and good-natured fun in the kaleidoscopic conversation, if one may so far mix metaphors, while the audience is awaiting the rise of the curtain, and in its course there is mention of a curious doubt:

'Do you know if there is to be any clapping of hands? —Can you tell me if it is allowable to say anything?'

It seems that at some private theatres loud demonstrations of applause were forbidden. It was thought more genteel to approve and admire in silence, thus to draw the line between professional actors and actresses, and gentlemen and lady performers. Upon trial, however, it had been found that the difference was sufficiently obvious, without marking it by any invidious distinction. Young and old amateurs have acknowledged that the silence, however genteel, was so dreadfully awful[1] that they preferred even the noise of vulgar exclamation. The cup of flattery was found so sweet that objections were no longer made to swallowing it in public.

Then follows a somewhat pedantic disquisition upon the fact that a certain Count Altenberg who is, with the prudence of many of Miss Edgeworth's heroes, *all but* in love with Caroline Percy, while a match with him is the one object of Georgiana Falconer's ambition, has come to the theatricals less with a view of civility and diversion than to study at leisure his *nearly* beloved's disposition, especially her behaviour while a rival is queening it on the stage and she herself is but one of the audience. Then we come

[1] Here seems a kind of harbinger to modern slang. The more usual slang words of Miss Edgeworth's time which corresponded to *awful* and *awfully* were *famous* and *famously*.

back to the play. Miss Falconer as Zara is easily first in merit. With the others

The faults common to unpractised actors occurred. One of Osman's arms never moved, and the other sawed the air perpetually, as if in pure despite of Hamlet's prohibition. Then, in crossing over, Osman was continually entangled in Zara's robe, or, when standing still, she was obliged to twitch her train thrice before she could get it from beneath his leaden feet. When confident that he could repeat a speech fluently, he was apt to turn his back upon his mistress, or when he felt himself called upon to listen to his mistress, he would regularly turn his back upon the audience. But all these are defects permitted by the license of a private theatre, allowable by courtesy to gentlemen actors; and things went on as well as could be expected. Osman had not his part by heart, but still Zara covered all deficiencies. And Osman did no worse than other Osmans had done before him, till he came to the long speech beginning:

> The Sultans, my great ancestors, bequeath'd
> Their empire to me, but their tastes they gave not.

Powerful prompting got him through the first six lines decently enough, till he came to

> . . . wasting tenderness in wild profusion.
> I might look down to my surrounded feet,
> And bless contending beauties.

At this he bungled sadly—his hearing suddenly failing as well as his memory there was a dead stop. In vain the prompter, the scene-shifter, the candle-snuffer, as loud as they could, and much louder than they ought, reiterated the next sentence:

> I might speak,
> Serenely slothful——

It was evident that Osman could not speak, nor was he

'serene.' He had begun, as in dangers great he was wont, to kick his left ancle-bone rapidly with his right heel; and through the pomp of Osman's oriental robes and turban young Petcalf stood confessed. He threw back an angry look at the prompter; Zara, terrified, gave up all for lost. The two Lady Arlingtons retreated behind the scenes to laugh. The polite audience struggled not to smile. Count Altenberg at this moment looked at Caroline, who, instead of joining in the laugh, showed by her countenance and manner the most good-natured sympathy. Zara, recovering her presence of mind, swept across the stage in such a manner as to hide from view her kicking Sultan; and as she passed she whispered the line to him so distinctly that he caught the sound, left off kicking, went on with his speech, and all was well again. Count Altenberg forgot to join in the cheering plaudits, he was so much charmed at that instant by Caroline's smile.

Fortunately for Zara, and for the audience, in the next scene the part of Lusignan was performed by a gentleman who had been well used to acting—though he was not a man of any extraordinary capacity, yet from his *habit of the boards*, and his being perfect in his part, he now seemed quite a superior person. It was found unaccountably easier to act with this son of labor than with any other of the gentlemen performers, though they were all natural geniuses.

All this, so far as the oddities of the performance are concerned, is excellently observed and excellently touched. The capital, perhaps the only, fault of the whole scene is found in the obtrusiveness with which the deficient good nature and good breeding of the Lady Arlingtons and of Miss Falconer are emphasised in order to show the beauties of Caroline Percy's character. This is pressed yet further after the passage just quoted. The Lady Arlingtons, jealous of Georgiana Falconer, have trained a little dog to answer to the name of *Osman*, in order that at the several repetitions of Osman's name in Zara's great speech the dog may rush on to the stage and wreak admired confusion. When the looked-for moment comes,

> Lady Frances, when she heard the reiterated and loud applause with which Zara was unanimously honoured, had felt half afraid to proceed in her scheme; but her companions observed that the scheme was so well concerted that everybody would suppose the entrance of the dog, and his exhibition, to be accidental, while, at the same time, it could not fail to make the audience laugh, at the very moment Miss Georgiana Falconer would wish them to weep.

So, when the supremely critical moment arrives, the dog

> ran on the stage, leaped up on Zara, and, at the repetition of his name, sat down on his hind legs, begged with his fore paws, and began to whine in such a manner that the whole audience were on the brink of laughter.—Caroline sprang forward, caught the dog in her arms, and carried him off the stage.—Count Altenberg, no longer master of himself, clapped his hands, and the whole house resounded with applause.

There is more in the same strain, all to the glorification of the immaculate Caroline Percy, whose triumphant issue from the tests decreed for her and for his own guidance by her singularly prudent lover is thus summed up. Miss Falconer, ignorant of the real cause for the clapping of hands, takes it to mean an *encore* for her speech (an odd idea ; though, to be sure, in later times Sothern's reading, as Dundreary, of Brother Sam's letter was often re-demanded) and begins all over again.

Caroline all the time kept the little dog quiet by her caresses, and Count Altenberg did not hear one word of the repetition of Zara's speech. At the beginning of the play, when the idea of trying Caroline's temper had occurred to him, he had felt some anxiety lest all the high ideas he had formed, all the bright enchantment should vanish. In the first act he had begun by joining timidly in the general applause of Zara, dreading lest Caroline should not be blessed with that temper which could bear the praises of a rival 'with unwounded ear.' But the Count applauded with more confidence in the second act, during the third was quite at his ease, and in the fifth could not forgive himself for having supposed it possible that Caroline could be liable to any of the foibles of her sex.

Now, through all the passages quoted, and through some omitted, the intention is almost painfully obvious to put Caroline Percy on a pedestal, to show her as a person superior to 'the foibles of her sex,' which are pushed forward with equal iteration in the characters of the Miss Falconers and the Lady Arlingtons. In Miss Austen's 'Mansfield Park' the ending of the vastly entertaining and characteristic rehearsals for private theatricals is to show that Fanny Price is superior not only to the foibles of her sex, but also to those displayed by members of the other sex, including even the admired Edmund, who on this occasion may be suspected of to some extent confusing the motives of wise temporising and of strong personal inclination. This one may say, that bringing into prominence the merits of Fanny Price, the story's heroine, is certainly the result of the way in which Miss Austen handles the theatrical scenes ; and that it was also, consciously or half consciously, the author's object may fairly be surmised. But the method here followed is unlike and by far preferable to that pursued by Miss Edgeworth, in that there is never an appearance of anxiety on the author's part to exalt the excellent qualities of her heroine, in whose quiet adherence to her own principles there is not a shadow of a shade of priggishness.

CHAPTER VIII

THE state of affairs, it will be remembered, in 'Mansfield Park' is this. Sir Thomas Bertram, of Mansfield Park, has taken a voyage to Antigua to look after an estate there. It is uncertain when he may return. The family party left behind him at the Park has had a reinforcement in the arrival, as a guest invited by Mr. Bertram, of 'the Honourable John Yates,' who 'had not much to recommend him beyond habits of fashion and expense.' Mr. Yates is stage-struck to the extent of a wild longing for showing on private stages how far superior he is to public performers. (In Miss Austen's day it was practically out of the question that a man of family should take to the stage as a profession.) He has just come from another country house, where intended private theatricals were inevitably put off by reason of a family bereavement—

To be so near happiness, so near fame, so near the long paragraph in praise of the private theatricals at Ecclesford, the seat of the Right Hon. Lord Ravenshaw, in Cornwall, which would of course have immortalised the whole party for at least a twelvemonth ! and being so near, to lose it all was an injury to be keenly felt, and Mr. Yates could talk of nothing else. . . . Happily for him, a love of the theatre is so general, an itch for acting so strong among young people, that he could hardly out-talk the interest of his hearers.

Therefore he goes easily off at score to describe what might and should have taken place. The play was 'Lovers' Vows' (a charmingly easy play for amateurs!), and Mr. Yates was to play Count Cassel—

'a trifling part and not at all to my taste, and such a one as I certainly would not accept again ; but I was determined to make no difficulties. [One has heard the selfsame thing said pretty frequently by private actors in our own days.] Lord Ravenshaw and the duke had appropriated the only two characters worth playing before I reached Ecclesford ; and though Lord Ravenshaw offered to resign his part to me, it was impossible to take it, you know. I was sorry for *him* that he should have so mistaken his powers, for he was no more equal to the Baron—a little man, with a weak voice, always hoarse after the first ten minutes. It must have injured the piece materially, but *I* was resolved to make no difficulties. Sir Henry thought the duke not equal to Frederick, but that was because Sir Henry wanted the part himself ; whereas it was certainly in the best hands of the two. I was surprised to see Sir Henry such a stick. Luckily the piece did not depend upon him. Our Agatha was inimitable, and the duke was thought very great by many. And upon the whole it would certainly have gone off wonderfully well.'

Now, there is nothing like this perfectly natural, perfectly selfish, and perfectly self-revealing speech from Mr. Yates to be found in the comedy of private theatricals, excellently as it is treated in the author's own way, given to us by Miss Edgeworth. With, assuredly, nothing wanting in actual perception of the curiosities evolved from the vanities and jealousies incident to amateur acting, Miss Edgeworth, nevertheless, did not here, or indeed elsewhere, show the peculiar quality of *fineness* that shows itself in every line of the speech just quoted from Miss Austen. In the analogous scenes in 'Patronage' Miss Edgeworth's colours, to borrow a metaphor from painting, are laid on 'with a good fat brush'—'fat' at least compared to that so exquisitely handled by Miss Austen. This author's method has been frequently likened to miniature-painting.[1] The comparison is sometimes misleading, because a too prevalent idea of miniature-painting is mere smallness. People sometimes forget that there was never a touch of 'niggling' in Cosway's work, and that, similarly, Miss Austen, writing within limits strictly self-imposed and observed, is never for a moment cramped.

But to continue—a proceeding for which no apology is needed—with specimens from the admirable passages devoted to the private theatricals at Mansfield Park. Tom Bertram, the eldest son, starts the idea of getting up theatricals by way of

[1] The comparison, it is true, has its origin in Miss Austen's own description of 'the little bit (two inches wide) of ivory on which I work with so fine a brush as produces little effect after so much labour.' This however was an intensely characteristic piece of true, but mistaken, modesty. If the amount of labour was not overrated, the 'effect' certainly seems to us extravagantly underrated.

consoling Mr. Yates, and it is warmly taken up by every one with a voice in the matter except Lady Bertram, who expresses no disapprobation—so indolent a person was not likely to do so—and Edmund Bertram, the younger son, who opposes the scheme, who is destined to the Church, but whose reasons for opposition are based solely on the facts that his father is away and in more or less constant danger, and that one of his sisters, being engaged to a stupid rich squire, Mr. Rushworth, shows the strongest disposition to flirt outrageously with Henry Crawford, a young man possessing both brains and money, who is staying hard by with his sister at the Vicarage. It has seemed worth while to mention particularly Edmund Bertram's reasons for objecting to the Mansfield Park theatricals, because one of Miss Austen's biographers and commentators has stated as a round fact that in 'Mansfield Park' Miss Austen 'infers decided disapproval of the amusement [theatricals].' Considering the frequent dramatic performances at Steventon with Madame de Feuillade, this is a startling statement; but then this is the same biographer who 'cannot imagine' Miss Austen 'greatly liked . . . out of the immediate circle of her friends' for the exquisite reason that, admirable gentlewoman as she was, she 'allowed her interests and sympathies to become *narrow*' [the italics are mine]. This is simply a puzzle; the mistake in the case of the play at Mansfield Park is explicable, though odd enough, since it takes no superhuman study to ascertain that what the author may be conceived, in agreement with Edmund Bertram, to disapprove, is not 'the amusement,' but the occasion and the play chosen. Edmund Bertram goes no farther than saying, apart from the reasons referred to, that 'in a *general* light, private theatricals are open to some objection.' He has before admitted being fond of 'real acting,' but 'would hardly walk from this room to the next to look at the raw efforts of those who have not been bred to the trade—a set of gentlemen and ladies, who have all the disadvantages of education and decorum to struggle through.' Here it will be noted that Miss Austen, if we are to suppose that she agrees with Edmund's sentiments, is at one with Miss Edgeworth, who in her own person as author relates how one performer in 'Zara' stood out from all the rest simply from 'the habit of the boards.'

Not the least delightful thing in the description of how the play is got up is the touch showing how at the very beginning Mr. Yates's ideas take a flight not contemplated even by Mr. Bertram, who however ends by falling in pretty closely with his friend's views.

'We must have a curtain,' said Tom Bertram ; 'a few yards of green baize for a curtain, and perhaps that may be enough.'

'Oh, quite enough,' cried Mr. Yates, 'with only just a side wing or two run up, doors in flat, and three or four scenes to let down ; nothing more would be necessary on such a plan as this. For mere amusement among ourselves we should want nothing more.'

This is excellent alike as a further exhibition of Mr. Yates's character, and as showing how such undertakings always gather magnitude as they progress. It is also interesting to note Miss Austen's curiously correct acquaintance with the terms of stage carpentry. It is not every reader nowadays, when things of stagecraft are more widely known than they were then, who would know at a glance the precise meaning of 'doors in flat.' When the play is at last decided on after much discussion (it is, it will be remembered, 'Lovers' Vows,' greatly to Edmund's dislike, and no wonder), the difficulties and jealousies about casting the parts are of course hit off with supreme skill; but this part is too long to quote in entirety, and to make snippets from it would be to serve no good purpose. It has been observed that, as in 'Patronage,' the circumstances serve to bring out the excellence of the heroine's character, but in 'Mansfield Park' the intention is never obtruded. The result seems to arise quite naturally from what is going on, and none of the characters particularly observe it either by chance, or, like Count Altenberg in 'Patronage,' with a purpose. Therefore the whole is like a scene or succession of scenes straight from nature, without the touch of pedantry which Miss Edgeworth often gave to her heroes and heroines, or that touch of caricature which the same author bestowed on some of her comic characters, and notably the two Clays, *French* and *English* Clay, in 'Patronage.' Mr. Rushworth, in 'Mansfield Park,' may be said to belong to broad comedy just as much as the two Clays, but then there is nothing overstrained in his description or in the behaviour ascribed to him. Like almost all Miss Austen's characters, he is a person whom one might meet at any moment in the dress of to-day. One of his speeches while the play is under discussion is practically the key to his nature, and in it one finds an instance of Miss Austen's extraordinary power of not only comprehending, but of making her readers comprehend, a whole character in a few delicate but firm touches.

'I should not have thought it the sort of play to be so easily filled up with us,' is observed, very wisely and properly, by Edmund Bertram.

'Mr. Rushworth followed him to say, "I come in three times, and have two-and-forty speeches. That's something, is not it? But I do not much like the idea of being so fine. I shall hardly know myself in a blue dress and a pink satin cloak."'

Mr. Rushworth has before dwelt, and continues afterwards to dwell, on his fine dress and his 'two-and-forty speeches,' but from the foregoing speech alone one sees him and realises him as completely as one does Sir Andrew Aguecheek by the time he has spoken barely more than a dozen words to Sir Toby Belch.

The characters of all the people concerned come out in the most perfect and natural way during the rehearsals of 'Lovers' Vows'—Mr. Bertram's idle, good-natured selfishness; Mr. Yates's vanity and want of proper feeling under a mask of fine breeding; Fanny's unselfishness and sincerity, and so on down to Mrs. Norris with her never-failing meanness, bullying of the unlucky Fanny, and pride in her own skill at 'contriving.' All is as though one actually saw and heard the personages, of which the pleasure is enhanced by our being allowed to see, and this without our attention being pushed or jogged, as through a clear magic glass, the secret motives and desires which inspire their every word and action. Certainly not the least effective part of the episode is the tragi-comic interruption of the rehearsals by Sir Thomas Bertram's sudden and unexpected return. Lady Bertram, good easy soul, presently lets out that the young people 'have been acting. We have been all alive with acting.' On his inquiring what they have been acting, Mr. Bertram glides over the matter by saying that they have been trying, 'by way of doing something and amusing my mother, to get up a few scenes—a mere trifle,' and then plunges deep into matters of pheasants and sport. But before long it becomes obvious that this pretext cannot last, since Sir Thomas proposes to look at 'his own dear room,' which has, as a matter of fact, been turned into a greenroom, being next to the billiard-room which has served for the theatre. Tom Bertram, hearing that Mr. Yates is alone in 'the theatre,' starts off at once to fetch him. He reaches the room 'just in time to witness the first meeting of his father and his friend. Sir Thomas had been a good deal surprised to find candles burning in his room; and, on casting his eye round it, to see other symptoms of recent habitation and a general air of confusion in the furniture. The removal of the book-case from before the billiard-room door struck him especially, but he had hardly more than time to feel astonished at all this, before there were sounds from the billiard-room to astonish him still further. Some one was talking there in a very loud accent—he did not know the voice—*more* than talking—almost hallooing. He stepped to the door, rejoicing at that moment in having the means of immediate communication, and, opening it, found himself on the stage of a theatre, and opposed to a ranting young man, who appeared likely to knock him down backwards. At the very moment of Yates perceiving Sir Thomas, and giving perhaps the very best start he had ever given in the whole course of his rehearsals, Tom Bertram entered at the other end of the room; and never had he found greater difficulty in keeping his countenance. His father's looks of solemnity and amazement on this his first appearance on any stage, and the gradual metamorphosis of the impassioned Baron Wildenheim into the well-bred and easy Mr. Yates, making his bow and apology to Sir Thomas Bertram, was such an exhibition, such a piece of true acting, as he would not have lost on any account. It would be the last—in all probability the last scene on that stage; but he was sure there could not be a finer. The house would close with the greatest éclat.'

For a sense of the truest comedy, comedy without a touch of farce or burlesque, this can no more be surpassed than can, in another way, the more serious touches which follow when Sir Thomas rejoins the family circle and seems, by his looks, to be particularly displeased with Edmund, on whose judgment, he appears to be thinking, he might surely have relied to prevent the theatrical scheme being entertained. The very brief but yet most full description here of Fanny's feelings, and the quiet dignity with which Sir Thomas intimates that there has been enough of acting, are small masterpieces.

The only contribution made by Miss Austen to dramatic literature, or at any rate the only one preserved, was written in her girlhood at Steventon. It has been quoted by more than one former commentator, but will, I think, bear quoting again. The manuscript ran thus:

THE MYSTERY:

An Unfinished Comedy.

Dedication to the Rev. George Austen.

Sir,—I humbly solicit your patronage to the following comedy, which, though an unfinished one, is, I flatter myself, as complete a *Mystery* as any of its kind.

I am, Sir, your most humble Servant,

The Author.

Dramatis Personæ.

Men	*Women*
Col. Elliott,	Fanny Elliott,
Old Humbug,	Mrs. Humbug, and
Young Humbug,	Daphne.
Sir Edward Spangle, and	
Corydon.	

ACT I.

SCENE I.—*A Garden.*

Enter CORYDON.

Corydon. But, hush ; I am interrupted.

[*Exit Corydon.*

Enter OLD HUMBUG *and his* Son, *talking.*

Old Hum. It is for that reason that I wish you to follow my advice. Are you convinced of its propriety?

Young Hum. I am, Sir, and will certainly act in the manner you have pointed out to me.

Old Hum. Then let us return to the house. [*Exeunt.*

SCENE II.—*A Parlour in* HUMBUG'S *house.*

MRS. HUMBUG *and* FANNY *discovered at work.*

Mrs. Hum. You understand me, my love?

Fanny. Perfectly, ma'am ; pray continue your narration.

Mrs. Hum. Alas! it is nearly concluded, for I have nothing more to say on the subject.

Fanny. Ah! here is Daphne.

Enter DAPHNE.

Daphne. My dear Mrs. Humbug, how d'ye do? Ah, Fanny, it is all over!

Fanny. Is it, indeed?

Mrs. Hum. I'm very sorry to hear it.

Fanny. Then 'twas to no purpose that I——

Daphne. None upon earth.

Mrs. Hum. And what is to become of——?

Daphne. Oh! 'tis all settled.

[*Whispers Mrs. Humbug.*]

Fanny. And how is it determined?

Daphne. I'll tell you. [*Whispers Fanny.*]

Mrs. Hum. And is he to——?

Daphne. I'll tell you all I know of the matter.

[*Whispers Mrs. Humbug and Fanny.*]

Fanny. Well, now I know everything about it I'll go away.

Mrs. Hum. and Daphne. And so will I. [*Exeunt.*

SCENE III.—*The curtain rises and discovers* Sir EDWARD SPANGLE, *reclined in an elegant attitude on a sofa, fast asleep.*

Enter Col. ELLIOTT.

Col. E. My daughter is not here, I see. There lies Sir Edward. Shall I tell him the secret? No, he'll certainly blab it. But he's asleep and won't hear me, so I'll e'en venture.

[*Goes up to Sir Edward, whispers him, and exit.*]

END OF THE FIRST ACT. FINIS.

This, for a skit, however fragmentary, upon a certain school of comedy written by a girl of fourteen or so is surely a most remarkable performance, bearing as it does a decided touch, in kind, of the same observation, wit, and humour finding expression in satire and burlesque that have made Canning's 'The Rovers, or the Double Arrangement' a possession for ever.

CHAPTER IX

WHAT was said in the very first lines of this little book may be with some modification repeated now, when one comes to consider Miss Austen's career and work by itself, without reference to other authors who were in the same sphere, although none of them can now be held an actual rival to a writer whose genius, if it dealt with interests less wide, was of a finer, more perfect, and more perfectly trained temper than any of theirs. So much has been written about Miss Austen's life, materials have been so eagerly sought, that almost all the little there is to tell has been already told. Her works have been envisaged from all kinds of points of view, and 'brief abstracts' of the stories and chief characters of the novels have been given by three authors[1] in a manner probably as satisfactory as such a method of treatment can reach. Those who desire compressed versions of Miss Austen's novels cannot do better than turn to one or all of the volumes mentioned in

[1] Mrs. Charles Malden (*Jane Austen.* London: Allen); Mr. O. F. Adams (*Chapters from Jane Austen.* Boston: Lee & Shepard); Professor Goldwin Smith (*Life of Jane Austen.* London: Walter Scott).

a footnote. Mr. Adams's volume is perhaps specially suited to a person who knows Miss Austen's works, but wishes to refresh his memory as quickly as possible, in that a commented list of *dramatis personæ* is prefixed to the short account of each novel. For the rest, though, as I have observed, there is scarcely anything new that can be said about Miss Austen's life, yet it may be both permissible and convenient to give a brief record of its events in special connection with the dates at which the novels were written and published.

I take the facts from the excellent memoir by the Rev. J. E. Austen Leigh, Miss Austen's nephew, published first in 1870, and subsequently with some important additions in the same volume with 'Lady Susan' and 'The Watsons' (of which more presently) in 1872. Both publications were put forth by Messrs. Bentley & Son.

Jane Austen was born on December 16, 1775, at the Parsonage House of Steventon in Hampshire. She was a daughter of the Rev. George Austen and Mrs. George Austen, who had been Miss Cassandra Leigh, daughter of the Rev. Thomas Leigh, of the Leighs of Warwickshire. The Austen family had been long established in the neighbourhood of Tenterden and Sevenoaks in Kent. Mr. George Austen, Jane's father, after having been at Tunbridge School and a Fellow of St. John's College, Oxford, came into possession of the Rectories, quite close to each other, of Deane and Steventon in Hampshire.

The former was purchased for him by the uncle, Mr. Francis Austen of Tunbridge, ancestor of the Austens of Kippington, who had taken charge of him as a boy of nine after his father's death. The latter was given to him by his cousin, Mr. Knight.

The Austens took up their abode at Steventon in 1771, and remained there about thirty years. The parsonage and grounds, some reminiscences of which probably appear in the novels, have been often described, and were first excellently described by Mr. J. E. Austen Leigh. Jane Austen had five brothers and one sister. The two youngest brothers, Francis and Charles, were sailors, 'during that glorious period of the British Navy,' when, as Mr. Austen Leigh observes, 'it was impossible for an officer to be almost always afloat, as these brothers were, without seeing service which, in these days, would be considered distinguished.' Accordingly there is not a flaw to be found in Miss Austen's treatment of matters concerning the Navy as it then was. The description, for instance, given by Lieutenant Price in 'Mansfield Park' of the 'Thrush' going out of harbour might well have been written by a sailor-novelist. Mr. Price, finding his sailor-son in 'the parlour,' welcomes him eagerly with

> 'Glad to see you. Have you heard the news? The "Thrush" went out of harbour this morning. Sharp is the word, you see. By G—, you are just in time. The doctor has been here inquiring for you; he has got one of the boats, and is to be off for Spithead by six, so you had

better go with him. I have been to Turner's about your mess; it is all in a way to be done. I should not wonder if you had your orders to-morrow; but you cannot sail with this wind, if you are to cruise to the westward; and Captain Webb certainly thinks you will have a cruise to the westward, with the "Elephant." By G—, I wish you may. But old Scholey was saying, just now, that he thought you would be sent first to the "Texel." Well, well, we are ready, whatever happens. But, by G—, you lost a fine sight by not being here in the morning to see the "Thrush" go out of harbour. I would not have been out of the way for a thousand pounds. Old Scholey ran in at breakfast-time, to say she had slipped her moorings and was coming out. I jumped up, and made but two steps to the platform. If ever there was a perfect beauty afloat, she is one; and there she lies at Spithead, and anybody in England would take her for an eight-and-twenty. I was upon the platform two hours this afternoon looking at her. She lies close to the "Endymion," between her and the "Cleopatra," just to the eastward of the sheer-hulk.'

To return to the habitat of the Austen family and the dates of the novels. It may be here mentioned that Jane Austen's sister Cassandra was some three years her senior. Cassandra was her chief or only confidante as to the plans and progress of the books, and, as Mr. Austen Leigh tells us, 'their sisterly affection for each other could hardly be exceeded.' At Steventon, besides 'Pride and Prejudice' and 'Sense and Sensibility,' 'Northanger Abbey' was composed in 1798, though not prepared for the press until 1803.

In 1801 'the family removed to Bath, where they

resided first at No. 4 Sydney Terrace, and afterwards in Green Park Buildings.' Here was written the unfinished story called 'The Watsons.' From Bath 'in the autumn of 1804 she spent some weeks at Lyme, and became acquainted with the Cobb, which she afterwards made memorable for the fall of Louisa Musgrove' [in 'Persuasion'].

In 1805 Mr. Austen died at Bath, when 'the widow and daughters went into lodgings for a few months, and then removed to Southampton,' where they lived in a corner house in Castle Square. In 1809 came the move to Chawton, where, between 1811 and 1816, were written 'Mansfield Park,' 'Emma,' and 'Persuasion.' The dates of publication of the novels were as follows: 'Sense and Sensibility' appeared in 1811, 'Pride and Prejudice' in 1813, 'Mansfield Park' in 1814, 'Emma' in 1816, 'Persuasion' and 'Northanger Abbey' in 1818, after the author's death. The history of 'Northanger Abbey' was very curious. It was in 1803 sold to a bookseller in Bath for ten pounds, and remained forgotten and neglected in this bookseller's drawers until one of Jane Austen's brothers bought it back for the same sum which had been given for it. When the transaction was completed he informed the doubtless astonished bibliopole that the work was by the author of 'Pride and Prejudice.' The last-named book is identified by Mr. Austen Leigh with the manuscript mentioned in a letter written in November 1797 by Miss Austen's father to Mr. Cadell the publisher:

'Sir,' he wrote, 'I have in my possession a manuscript novel, comprising 3 vols., about the length of Miss Burney's 'Evelina.' As I am well aware of what consequence it is that a work of this sort sh[d] make its first appearance under a respectable name, I apply to you. I shall be much obliged therefore if you will inform me whether you choose to be concerned in it, what will be the expense of publishing it at the author's risk, and what you will venture to advance for the property of it, if on perusal it is approved of. Should you give any encouragement I will send you the work.

'I am, Sir, your humble servant,

'GEORGE AUSTEN.'

By return of post Mr. Cadell wrote declining to have anything to do with the work.

Comment has often been made, and most justly made, on the perfect breeding and manners of those people in Miss Austen's novels who are supposed and intended to be well bred. The frequent reference to Chawton in this chapter leads me to think it a suitable place for introducing to the reader two letters hitherto unpublished, although allusion is made to them by Lord Brabourne. The object in quoting them is to show in what a perfect atmosphere of the truest dignity and good feeling Miss Austen passed her life. The letters were exchanged between Miss Austen's second brother, Edward, who 'was early adopted by his cousin, Mr. Knight, of Godmersham Park in Kent and Chawton House in Hampshire,' and Mrs. Knight, then a widow. Edward, it may be remembered, took the name of Knight. The letters practically explain themselves :

My dearest Madam,—I went to Bed last Night fully determined on paying you an early visit this morning in consequence of two letters of yours to Mr. Deedes, which he yesterday gave me to peruse, but the more I have thought of it the less I find myself capable of conversing with you on so extraordinary and important a subject. I have therefore determined to make use of my pen, tho' I am confident I shall even then fall very short of expressing half what I feel at the moment I am writing. It is impossible, my dst. Madam, for anyone to have a higher sense of your unlimited Bounty and kindness to me than both Elizth and myself; were we not truly sensible of it we should indeed be the most ungratefull of Beings, but I trust and indeed know you are convinced of the sincerity of our Gratitude and Affection. Believe me, therefore, my dear Madam, equally sincere when I say it is impossible for us in this Instance to accede to your Plan. I am confident we should never be happy at Godmersham whilst you were living at a smaller and less comfortable House—or in reflecting that you had quitted your own favourite Mansion, where I have so often heard you say your whole Happiness was center'd, and had retired to a residence and style of Living to which you have been ever unaccustomed, and this to enrich us. We are, believe me, thanks to your continued Bounties, comfortable and happy; nor do I know how that Happiness can be better continued than by seeing you in a Situation where I know you must be more comfortable than any alteration can possibly make you. You will, therefore, my d^{r} Madam, not think us ungratefull if I again repeat my wishes that you abandon your present plan—the remembrance of it will be cordially engraved on our Minds; our

Feelings I will not endeavour to express.—I shall now take an early opportunity of seeing you ; till then, adieu !

EDWD. AUSTEN.

ROWLING : Nov. 23, 1797.

Sale Park : Friday.

If anything were wanting, my dearest Edward, to confirm my resolution concerning the plan I propose executing, your Letter would have that effect ; it is impossible for any person to express their gratitude and affection in terms more pleasing and gratifying than you have chosen, and from the bottom of my heart I believe you to be perfectly sincere when you assure me that your happiness is but secured by seeing me in the full enjoyment of every thing that can contribute to my ease and comfort, and that happiness, my dear Edward, will be yours by acceding to my wishes. From the time that my partiality for you induced Mr. Knight to treat you as our adopted child I have felt for you the tenderness of a Mother, and never have you appeared more deserving of affection than at this time ; to reward your merit, therefore, and to place you in a situation where your many excellent qualities will be call'd forth and render'd useful to the neighbourhood, is the fondest wish of my heart. Many circumstances attached to large landed Possessions, highly gratifying to a Man, are entirely lost on me at present ; but when I see you in the enjoyment of them, I shall, if possible, feel my gratitude to my beloved Husband redoubled, for having placed in my hands the power of bestowing happiness on one so very dear to me. If my Income had not been sufficient to enable us both to live in affluence, I never shd. have proposed this plan, for nothing would have given me more pain than to have seen a rigid economy take place of that liberality which y[e] poor have always experienced from this family ; but wth the

Income I have assigned you, I trust, my dear Ed[d], you will feel yourself rich. You must be satisfied however on this head ; and I hope you will very soon come over, when you shall inspect every account I have, and form your own judgment. As I have no letter from Mr. Deedes I conclude he has not heard from Forster. I hope there will be no difficulty in arranging the Plan. You will see by one of my Letters to Mr. D—— that I am desirous of making the Deed irrevocable, during your life ; for your being kept in a state of dependance on my wish, or perhaps caprice, would not be less painful to you, than disagreeable to myself. But if Mr. Deedes should be of opinion that a promise under my own hand, as binding as words can make it and deliver'd one to you and another to the Trustees, would be sufficient for your necessity, and save some trouble, I shall not object to such a Mode; but this and many other points we can discuss when I see you. You will observe, my dear Edward, that I depend on your obedience to my wish, and assure yourself and my dear Lizzie, that the sacrifice I make is far from being so great as you imagine ; the emolument of a great Income is no object to me, for reasons I have already stated to Mr. Deedes, and even the pain I shall feel in quitting this dear Place will no longer be remembered when I see you in possession of it. My attachment to it can, I think, only cease with my life; but if I am near enough to be your frequent daily visitor, and within reach of the side of you and your Boys, and Lizzie and her Girls, I trust I shall be as happy, perhaps happier than I am now.—A plan so important to us both, you may imagine, I have not adopted without being convinced on this point; my judgment has been unbiassed, for as it was a subject of too much delicacy for anyone to offer advice upon, and as I had determined how to act, I forbore to mention it, and even Harriet did not know it, till a few days before I wrote to Mr. Deedes.

Adieu, my dearest Edward, and believe me to be, with the truest affection for you and yrs,

Y^{r} most sincere friend,

C. K.

There is surely something singularly touching in the sincere affection and the delightful courtesy of this correspondence, and it is certainly most characteristic of the race to which Miss Austen belonged.

Jane Austen

CHAPTER X

MENTION has been made in a previous chapter of the one slip in Miss Austen's accuracy in observation and description of features in landscape. This slip occurs in 'Emma,' where, to quote again from my father's article in 'Fraser,' at almost midsummer

> Strawberries are described as being eaten from the beds at Donwell Abbey, while the orchard is in blossom at the neighbouring Abbey Mill Farm—an anachronism which we have never met with any horticulturist able to explain by bringing together even the earliest and latest varieties of apple and strawberry.

The passage in question runs thus: Emma, when the party are on their way to see the view of Abbey Mill Farm from Donwell, perceives 'Mr. Knightley and Harriet distinct from the rest, quietly leading the way.' There had been a time when Harriet Smith and Mr. Knightley were not likely to be companions, and when Emma would have been sorry Harriet should see so favourable a view of Abbey Mill Farm. However, a young farmer wishes to marry, and finally does marry, Harriet Smith; but at first this is a most displeasing idea to Emma, who has 'taken up'

Harriet, and thinks, foolishly, that she ought to do better. 'Now' Abbey Mill Farm 'might be safely viewed with all its appendages of prosperity and beauty, its rich pastures, spreading flocks, *orchard* in *blossom*, and light column of smoke ascending.' With regard to this I find, on the fly-leaf at the end of the volume in which the article on 'British Novelists' is bound up, the following copy, in my father's handwriting, of a letter written by Miss Caroline Austen, niece to Jane :

Ferog Firle.

MY DEAREST CHARLOTTE,—There is a tradition in the family respecting the apple-blossom as seen from Donwell Abbey on the occasion of the strawberry party, and it runs thus—That the first time my uncle Knight [this was the first Mr. Edward Knight of Chawton House] saw his sister after the publication of 'Emma' he said, 'Jane, I wish you would tell me where you get those apple-trees of yours that come into bloom in July.' In truth she did make a mistake--there is no denying it—and she was speedily apprised of it by her brother—but I suppose it was not thought of sufficient consequence to call for correction in a later edition.

Mr. W. Austen Leigh writes to me that 'the *Charlotte* to whom my aunt wrote must, we think, have been Charlotte Warren—a school friend. She afterwards became Mrs. Roberts, and was the mother of the Margaret Roberts who wrote "Mademoiselle Mori."'

The slip on Miss Austen's part is certainly very curious, but how very much more curious is it that it should be the only slip in accurate observation which has ever been pointed out in the works of an author whose first (and, as some good judges think, best) novel was written when she was but one-and-twenty! I suppose that so many admirers and lovers of Miss Austen's work as there may be, almost as many different opinions as to the order of merit in which her novels should be placed might be discovered. The question is not a very easy one to decide according to purely critical methods; and as criticism is not an exact science, in many cases the preference must be an altogether personal feeling—that is, it must be a matter of opinion rather than of criticism, two things which are far too frequently confused. There is, to be sure, an obvious method of avoiding the greatest difficulties involved in comparison between the novels by lumping together two or three or four as superior to the others, and there leaving the matter. But that appears unsatisfactory and otiose. It seems to me, however, safe to suppose that not many readers would be inclined on any grounds to give the very first place to 'Sense and Sensibility.' The circumstances, recounted in a former chapter, in which this novel was written are quite enough to account for the fact that to many devoted admirers of Miss Austen, including myself, it appears decidedly the least considerable of the six novels on which rests the fame of that great novelist. As its first beginning was, clearly enough, the first inception of the scheme adopted in 'Pride and Prejudice,' so it is only natural that when this beginning was amplified and finished the whole should look, as I have said, something like a curious shadow of its predecessor in complete writing (not in publication), though not in idea. It is supposed, and perhaps justly, that all authors of fiction in the first rank have an unquenchable love, as mothers have, for their really first offspring, and I think the completion and publication of 'Sense and Sensibility' may be quoted in support of this idea. I find myself in accord with Mr. Austin Dobson as to the belief that no 'Austenite' would rank 'Sense and Sensibility' along with 'Emma,' 'Pride and Prejudice,' or 'Northanger Abbey,' and certainly no man can desire a better or surer support to his own opinion than the judgment of Mr. Austin Dobson. It is true that in 'Sense and Sensibility' there is one most excellent original character—the vulgar, genial, match-making Mrs. Jennings. But for the rest they can all be matched more or less from the other novels, with one exception. To take an instance of repetition, what is Willoughby but a sort of reflection of Wickham in 'Pride and Prejudice'? To be sure Wickham was 'an out-and-outer,' while Willoughby has redeeming points, but the informing idea is the same in both characters. It is in deference to Mr. Dobson's judgment that I have noted the exception. This is found, by him, in the character of Mr. Robert Ferrars, 'that egregious amateur in tooth-pick cases.' But does not Mr. Robert Ferrars somehow recall, not another character of Miss Austen's, but two at least of Miss Burney's—the languid yet swaggering dandies who appear in 'Evelina' and in 'Camilla'?

Mr. Austin Dobson makes yet another exception in favour of 'the admirably matched Mr. and Mrs. John Dashwood.' Well, no doubt they are not only admirably matched, but also admirably drawn; and the scene to which Mr. Austin Dobson specially refers, wherein between them they—Mrs. John Dashwood being the instigator—cut down Mr. John Dashwood's originally generous intentions towards Mrs. Dashwood and her daughters to a mere nothing, is in itself a perfection of insight and execution. It can be paralleled, so far as I know, only by the scene in Sir Walter Besant's 'The Seamy Side,' where Stephen Hamblin, sitting by himself in what he vainly thinks his ill-acquired house, goes through the same process of consideration with regard to his niece. Mr. Adams, the American author before quoted in these pages, was singularly well inspired when he wrote that in certain characteristics Anthony Trollope among more modern novelists came nearest to Miss Austen. I think that, for many passages in his works, Sir Walter Besant might be included in the comparison; but I imagine that his fame was not established, nor his full merit known, as it now is, when Mr. Adams wrote.

To return, however, to the John Dashwoods. Without venturing to contradict Mr. Austin Dobson, I yet think that the quality of 'sordidness' which he himself mentions as belonging to the Miss Steeles in the same book, prevents one from ranking Mr. and Mrs. John Dashwood among the really happiest of Miss Austen's achievements. Compare them, to take an example, with Mrs. Norris in 'Mansfield Park,' who is quite as sordid as were the John Dashwoods. Yet who rises from reading of Mrs. Norris with a bitter taste in his mouth, and who does not rise with such a taste in his mouth from reading of the John Dashwoods? It would appear—at least it appears to me—that, when she wrote 'Sense and Sensibility,' Miss Austen had not fully developed that fine, that exquisite sense of humour which makes us more than tolerate in fiction the self-revelations of people whose characteristics in real life would annoy or shock, or both. Prince Hal when he came to his own would no more of Falstaff. Yet what reader is there who does not always retain a sneaking kindness for fat Jack? One has, of course, in that sense no sneaking kindness for Mrs. Norris, who is frankly detestable if you look into her character as you might into that of a person whom you were liable to meet any and every day. Yet, again, can you find a more amusing companion than she is in Miss Austen's pages? The fact, in other words, would seem to be that the John Dashwoods suffered from excess of *realism*—a word, I think, not invented or current in Miss Austen's day, but it serves well to express what I mean.

It is clear from several passages in the 'Fraser' article that my father—than whom it would have been hard to find a more devoted 'Austenite' or a better equipped critic—viewed 'Sense and Sensibility' with considerably more favour than it finds in the eyes of most critics of anything like his own calibre. And I must confess that my own opinion leans to theirs. I think, in fine, that in considering any question of precedence in Miss Austen's six novels we may really 'count out' 'Sense and Sensibility.'

Her Contemporaries and Herself

CHAPTER XI

TURNING for the hundredth, or probably more than hundredth, time for instruction and pleasure to Mr. Austin Dobson's most excellent introductions to Miss Austen's novels in Messrs. Macmillan's edition, I find myself face to face with an extremely rare experience—that of discovering a slip on Mr. Austin Dobson's part. The matter is thus. In the Introduction to 'Pride and Prejudice' Mr. Austin Dobson writes: 'Before she had thus transformed her earliest story ['Elinor and Marianne,' rechristened after revision 'Sense and Sensibility'] she had completed the novel which, by universal consent, is regarded as her masterpiece—"Pride and Prejudice."' On the other hand, in the Introduction to 'Sense and Sensibility,' Mr. Dobson, premising that this cannot be called Miss Austen's greatest novel, goes on to say 'there are who swear by "Persuasion;" there are who prefer "Emma" and "Mansfield Park;" there is a large contingent for "Pride and Prejudice;" and there is even a section which advocates the pre-eminence of "Northanger Abbey."' Well, this is certainly in contradiction to the other statement that 'Pride and Prejudice' 'is regarded by universal consent' as the author's 'masterpiece.' This is really a mighty small matter, but it naturally leads one to considering whether 'Northanger Abbey' should or not be ranked as having an equal claim with 'Emma' and 'Pride and Prejudice.' There is certainly a strong point in its favour, that, as we have seen, it divided with 'Emma' Sir Walter Scott's special affection and attention. Personally, I cannot think it equal as a 'complete, finished, rounded-off' piece of work to 'Emma' or 'Pride and Prejudice,' and that largely for reasons so clearly put by Mr. Austin Dobson that I may be permitted to give them in his own words :

Miss Austen, as we know, in her girlish efforts, had amused herself by ridiculing the silly romances of the circulating library, and it is probable that 'Northanger Abbey' was originally only a more serious and sustained attempt to do for the Radcliffe school what Cervantes had done for 'Esplaudian' and 'Florismarte of Hyrcania,' and Mrs. Lenox for 'Cassandra' and 'Cleopatra.' But the ironical treatment is not always apparent, and there are indications that, as often happens, the author's growing interest in the characters diverts her insensibly from her purpose. There are, besides, passages, such as the spirited defence of novels at the end of chapter v., with its odd *boutade* against the 'Spectator,' which have a look of afterthought, and it is not very unreasonable to assume that, setting out with a purely satiric intent, Miss Austen ultimately moved in a diagonal between a study in irony and a story. One result of this is that, her attention not being wholly confined to the creation of character, her third novel (in the order of writing) contains no personage corresponding to Mr. Collins, or to the Mrs. Norris of her next book But Mrs. Allen is 'perfectly well' (as Gray would say) in her colourless kind; and as a mere study there is nothing anywhere to approach, in its vivid fidelity, that extremely objectionable specimen of the horsey university man of the Gillray and Rowlandson eras, Mr. John Thorpe, who, it may be noted, admires Mrs. Radcliffe and abuses Miss Burney.

All this seems to me as true as it is well expressed, and, if we grant its truth, 'Northanger Abbey,' full as it is of admirable touches in depicting character, scenery, and manners, can hardly claim any right to the first place or a division of the first place among the novels. Nor on second thoughts, perhaps, has Sir Walter Scott's affection for the book any real reference to this particular question. I know many lovers of Miss Austen, and count myself among them, who, having read 'Northanger Abbey' through a great number of times, can now take it up in any spare moment and feel sure of happening almost immediately upon some delightful passage. The case might be paralleled from other great authors, notably Mr. Thackeray; and I take it that Sir Walter Scott's love for the book may have been rather of this kind than the result of a purely critical opinion. Such an opinion can, I think, be applied to 'Northanger Abbey' in reference to the other novels, on the very grounds as to which I have quoted Mr. Austin Dobson. That 'moving in a diagonal' to which he refers cannot but produce, after a sustained reading of the book, a certain impression of patchiness which is never derived from a like harking back to 'Emma,' 'Pride and Prejudice,' or 'Mansfield Park.' And thus the preference of these three to 'Northanger Abbey' may perhaps be accounted a matter of criticism, and not of mere personal opinion. To say that the book has a charm entirely its own is to say that Miss Austen wrote it. But beyond the 'diagonal movement' some of the characters and incidents are, it may be thought, just a trifle out of that perfect harmony to which Miss Ellis has so gracefully referred. While the Thorpes are inimitable, and the Tilneys, brother and sister, are, like Mrs. Allen, 'perfectly well,' there is surely a touch of extravagance in General Tilney's absolutely brutal behaviour in packing Catherine off, without a carriage or a servant provided for her safety and comfort, the moment he discovers that his ideas, borrowed from the ill-bred inventions of John Thorpe, as to Catherine's prospective wealth, are completely unfounded in fact. Then, to take an instance, the exploration by Catherine (in which, or rather directly after which, she is surprised by Henry Tilney) of the late Mrs. Tilney's room, where Catherine vainly imagines there may be some clue to a horrid mystery after the manner of Mrs. Radcliffe—this surely is a little overcharged, just as Henry Tilney's behaviour and hers on the occasion are open to doubt. It was hardly his business to pry into Catherine's motives for a somewhat unwarrantable voyage of discovery; and she was hardly such a fool as so very needlessly and indiscreetly to reveal her silly imaginings. Here, as elsewhere in this book and as nowhere else in the novels, Miss Austen is clearly playing an ironical chorus to her own characters; but there is a further inference to be drawn from the whole passage. Mr. Austin Dobson has proved his point, were material proof needed, about the retouching, by a reference to Miss Edgeworth's 'Belinda.' In chapter v. this novel is mentioned by name for a special purpose, and Mr. Austin Dobson shows by comparison of dates, in a footnote to his Introduction, that this mention cannot well have existed in the first draft of the book, since 'Belinda' was not published until 1801, whereas 'Northanger Abbey' was first composed in 1798, the year after the first appearance of Mrs. Radcliffe's 'The Italian.' I find marks, though I have no such proof to back my impression, of the same retouching in this scene between Catherine Morland and Henry Tilney. It may probably have been designed originally on the same purely satiric lines that we find in the description of Catherine's first experience with the mysterious cabinet and the mysterious document, which turns out to be a washing bill, at Northanger Abbey, and have suffered a change as the characters ran away with their author's first intention. I believe that any one thoroughly well up in Miss Austen's work, if the idea has not occurred to her or him before, will, after carefully re-reading the passage (chapter xxiv. 'Northanger Abbey'), be inclined to my opinion.

The other passage which gives occasion for Mr. Austin Dobson's footnote is unique, and therefore worth quoting. I cannot recall any other point in any of the novels where Miss Austen so unreservedly expresses, speaking in her own person, her individual opinions, one of which (about the 'Spectator') is, as Mr. Dobson has noted, a little out of the way:

The progress of the friendship between Catherine [Morland] and Isabella [Thorpe] was quick as its beginning had been warm; and they passed so rapidly through every gradation of increasing tenderness, that there was shortly no fresh proof of it to be given to their friends or themselves. They called each other by their Christian name, were always arm in arm when they walked, pinned up each other's dress for the dance, and were not to be divided in the set; and, if a rainy morning deprived them of other enjoyments, they were still resolute in meeting, in defiance of wet and dirt, and shut themselves up to read novels together. Yes, novels; for I will not adopt that ungenerous and impolitic custom, so common with novel-writers, of degrading, by their contemptuous censure, the very performances to the number of which they are themselves adding; joining with their greatest enemies in bestowing the harshest epithets on such works, and scarcely ever permitting them to be read by their own heroine, who, if she accidentally take up a novel, is sure to turn over its insipid pages with disgust. Alas! if the heroine of one novel be not patronised by the heroine of another, from whom can she expect protection and regard? I cannot approve of it. Let us leave it to the reviewers to abuse such effusion of fancy at their leisure, and over every new novel to talk in threadbare strains of the trash with which the press now groans. Let us not desert one another—we are an injured body. Although our productions have afforded more extensive and unaffected pleasure than those of any other literary corporation in the world, no species of composition has been so much decried. From pride, ignorance, or fashion, our foes are almost as many as our readers; and while the abilities of the nine-hundredth abridger of the History of England, or of the man who collects and publishes in a volume some dozen lines of Milton, Pope, and Prior, with a paper from the 'Spectator,' and a chapter from Sterne, are eulogised by a thousand pens,—there seems almost a general wish of decrying the capacity and undervaluing the labour of the novelist, and of slighting the performances which have only genius, wit, and taste to recommend them. 'I am no novel-reader—I seldom look into novels—Do not imagine that *I* often read novels—It is really very well for a novel.' Such is the common cant. 'And what are you reading, Miss ——?' 'Eh! it is only a novel,' replies the young lady; while she lays down her book with affected indifference, or momentary shame. 'It is only "Cecilia," or "Camilla" [Miss Austen was ever loyal], or "Belinda;"' or, in short, only some work in which the greatest powers of the mind are displayed, in which the most thorough knowledge of human nature, the happiest delineation of its varieties, the liveliest effusions of wit and humour, are conveyed to the world in the best-chosen language.[1] Now, had the same young lady been engaged with a volume of the 'Spectator,' instead of such a work, how proudly would she have produced the book, and told its name! though the chances must be against her being occupied by any part of that voluminous publication of which either the matter or manner would not disgust a young person of taste; the substance of its papers so often consisting in the statement of improbable

[1] Could there be a more charmingly unconscious description of Miss Austen's own novels?

circumstances, unnatural characters, and topics of conversation, which no longer concern any one living; and their language, too, frequently so coarse as to give no very favourable idea of the age that could endure it.

Now this is a divagation most certainly unique in kind in Miss Austen's work. Therefore it is the more valuable in a sense. Yet, following for my own part the line I have indicated, I find that its very presence, loth as one would be to part with it, is one of the causes that make the workmanship of 'Northanger Abbey' defective. It really has no reason for being found where it is better than a desire on the author's part to 'let off' that mere scintilla of discontent with things as they are, which was the nearest approach Miss Austen could make, in public or private, to ill-humour. And yet how true it was, in the main, at the time when it was written! What one greatly desires to know is, who were the particular novelists that abused their brethren and sisters in the art? If any one knows, Mr. Austin Dobson does; but he has given no sign, and I wish he had. Not the less, greatly as I affect 'Northanger Abbey,' do I potently and powerfully agree with him, as on possibly more important points, so on this following one. 'Personally,' he writes, 'we could willingly have surrendered a good deal of the clever raillery about Mrs. Radcliffe for a little more of Beau Nash's old city, which Miss Austen knew so thoroughly. But her nice sense of artistic restraint docs not admit of this.' One may have personal regret, but though the artistic sense fails to dominate the 'diagonal movement,' and permits such an excursus as that just quoted—just because there is plenty of evidence of artistic sense running untrammelled all through the book, what true 'Austenite' could wish 'Northanger Abbey' to be other than it is?

CHAPTER XII

'PERSUASION,' Professor Goldwin Smith writes in his 'Life of Jane Austen,' 'has had passionate admirers in two persons not unqualified to judge—Miss Martineau and Miss Mitford.' To these opinions may be added that of Dr. Whewell, quoted by Mrs. Charles Malden, that '"Persuasion" is the most beautiful of all Jane Austen's stories.' To this dictum Mrs. Malden herself gave more or less—rather more than less—adherence, and Professor Goldwin Smith gives it as his critical opinion that 'though as a whole not so well constructed as others of Jane Austen's novels, it may be said to contain the finest touches of her art.' With this statement I cannot any more completely agree than I can with that to which I have before referred as to the 'overdrawing' of Sir Walter Elliot's conceit. The merits of characterisation and description in 'Persuasion' are unquestionable, and the intention is as clear as it is in any other of the novels. Yet—and here I think one touches on personal opinion, and not on criticism properly so called—it seems to me to lack the thoroughly sustained interest of 'Emma,' 'Pride and Prejudice,' and 'Mansfield Park.' The book has, as has been pointed out by more than one writer, a peculiar attraction, if attraction is the right word, in the shade of pensiveness and tender melancholy which may have been due to the author's declining health. It was her last work, her swan-song; and though it certainly is not deficient in either wit or humour, it has, as it were, an atmosphere of regret that does not belong to the other books. It ends happily. Anne Elliot, whom Professor Goldwin Smith finds 'the most interesting of Jane Austen's women,' marries, after weary years of disappointment (partly her own fault), the man of her choice, a very excellent person, and poetic justice is dealt out all round. But in spite of this happy final adjustment the whole book has what might be called a cadence of sadness. This I do not point to as a defect, but as a peculiarity which marks it out from the author's other work. The shortcomings—need I explain that I venture on such a word only by way of comparison with some of Miss Austen's other novels?—appear to me to lie first in the matter mentioned by Professor Goldwin Smith of a somewhat faulty construction. In the second place, I infinitely prefer Elizabeth Bennet and Emma to Anne Elliot; but this, considering that both Mr. Austin Dobson and Professor Goldwin Smith are dead against me, must be dismissed as being simply personal prejudice. And yet, in some kind of support for this prejudice, I may be allowed to quote from Miss Austen herself, who, in 1816, wrote to her niece: 'You may, *perhaps*, like the heroine, as she is almost too good for me.' There is, indeed, the only excuse for not being more interested than one might or ought to be in Anne Elliot. A touch of imperfection would surely emphasise rather than obscure her excellent qualities—such a touch, for instance, as Emma's one lapse from good feeling and, it must be added, good breeding, when she 'quizzes' Miss Bates's garrulity so openly that even the kind-hearted grateful old lady herself does not fail to feel the sting of a thoughtless speech. Yet, I must repeat, I must not set myself against such excellent judges as have pronounced in favour of Anne Elliot I can only regret that, no doubt from defective literary vision, I prefer, for company, even Catherine Morland, in 'Northanger Abbey,' who is described, oddly as it seems to me, by one commentator of Miss Austen as 'an obvious copy of "Evelina;" a good-hearted, simple-minded little goose.'

I cannot think that either Catherine Morland or Miss Burney's Evelina can be justly described as a 'goose.' Simple-minded, yes. Girls in that time were simple-minded. The New Woman as yet was not. All through Miss Austen's work, as through Miss Burney's, one finds very well marked the sense that a girl must not think of a man as a possible lover and, consequently, husband, until the man has given unequivocal signs of his partiality. It was considered immodest. Perhaps it ought to be so considered still. Perhaps it ought not to be so considered. That is a question of Ethics. What is certain is that we must look at Miss Austen's heroines from that point of view—that no inclination towards an aspiring swain was to be admitted even in the heroine's own heart. Least of all was she to admit any preference to any member of her family or any of her intimate friends or acquaintance. A sly hint as to a growing attachment was always to be met with a rebuke which, to be sure, was sometimes as in the case of Jane and Bingley in 'Pride and Prejudice,' more a veil of convention than a true expression of feeling. This state of things, in Miss Austen's day, is perhaps too little remembered. There it was, beyond all doubt; and from Sir Thomas Bertram's displeasure (in 'Mansfield Park') at Fanny Price's refusal to become the wife of Henry Crawford one gets the idea that, in Miss Austen's time and among the people whom she so marvellously depicts, the question of marriage was more usually regarded as an affair of business and convenience than is the case, generally, in the corresponding circles of the present day. Marriages of convenience have been always made, and will probably continue to be made so long as 'this needy planet' endures. Yet, the feeling as to marriage was surely not quite the same in Miss Austen's day as now.

To be sure, in a certain sense Darcy's marriage with Eliza Bennet might be called a marriage of affection or love, but then both the man and the maid took such a very long time to make up their minds! Bingley's marriage with Jane, in the same novel, seems to me a matter of less consideration as regards the particular point. Bingley was 'an agreeable rattle,' and Jane was a somewhat studious (in the best sense) and stately person. Therefore Miss Austen perceived that they ought to make a match, and made it so. The more readily perhaps because one was more than affluent, while the other was not an absolute pauper. Neither of these marriages, I have said, can be strictly called either *de convenance* or a marriage solely of first inclination. The same book however contains an instance of an absolute love-match between Wickham and Lydia, of which, as will be remembered, the results were not encouraging. This is one of the points in Miss Austen's novels that have always impressed me strongly. The cloak of a somewhat strained propriety was then so much more frequently invoked than it is now, that I believe nothing short of the amazing delicacy of Miss Austen's touch would have induced the then reading public to accept without protest the incident of an illegalised elopement. Be that as it may, I should have always felt certain, even without the hints given by Miss Austen, that Wickham and Lydia lived *un*happily ever after.

These considerations have however distracted me from the scene (in 'Mansfield Park') which may be regarded as the *locus classicus* in Miss Austen as to the view taken by a somewhat severe but by no means unkindly guardian of the proper attitude of mind to be taken by a 'young person' on the marriage question. The position is this. Sir Thomas Bertram has received a proposal for the hand of his niece (by marriage), Fanny Price, from the rich and accomplished Henry Crawford. Fanny has many reasons for dreading a marriage with Crawford. At one point in the conversation between oddly matched interlocutors—a conversation not the less instinct with vivacity and truth to character—Sir Thomas asks her :

'Have you any reason, child, to think ill of Mr. Crawford's temper?'

She replies, 'No, sir.'

Miss Austen continues: 'She longed to add, "But of his principles I have," but her heart sank under the appalling prospect of discussion, explanation, and probably non-conviction.' Sir Thomas, clear in the conviction that his ward should adopt *his*, not *her*, views as to a suitable match, continues his part of the old-fashioned guardian, and finally ends a long speech, replete with admonitions as to a 'young person's' duty in this regard, with these very unpleasant words :

'. . . let me tell you, Fanny, that you may live eighteen years longer in the world, without being addressed by a man of half Mr. Crawford's estate, or a tenth part of his merits. Gladly would I have bestowed either of my own daughters on him. Maria is nobly married [here comes out Miss Austen's fine sense of irony], but had Mr. Crawford sought Julia's hand, I should have given it to him ['given it to him' is characteristic] with superior and more heartfelt satisfaction than I gave Maria's to Mr. Rushworth.'

Here again, seeing what happened afterwards, one recognises what a distinguished Frenchman once called 'that very little and important thing, genius,' in Miss Austen's method. She had, I cannot doubt, arranged the subsequent catastrophe in her own mind before she put these pompous, useless words into Sir Thomas's mouth. Sir Thomas goes on:

'I should have been very much surprised had either of my daughters, on receiving a proposal of marriage at any time, which might carry with it only *half* the eligibility of *this*, immediately and peremptorily, and without paying my opinion or my regard the compliment of any consideration, put a decided negative on it. I should have been much surprised and much hurt, by such a proceeding. I should have thought it a gross violation of duty and respect. *You* are not to be judged by the same rules. You do not owe me the duty of a child. But, Fanny, if your heart can acquit you of *ingratitude*——'

Here poor Fanny naturally breaks down, and, another touch of truth, Sir Thomas gradually relents as far as such a man could relent.

It is not certain that the more modern ways have made marriage a more perfect institution than it was when matches were arranged according to the ideas of Sir Thomas Bertram. But the difference is worth notice. In a modern novel the coercion applied to Fanny Price and to Anne Elliot (in 'Persuasion') would, if described at all, be accompanied with comments upon its want of kindness and consideration. In Miss Austen's times, in contrast to the good feeling and courtesy shown in two letters I have quoted, the father or uncle was, if not a tyrant, at least a despot as regarded his feminine belongings. It does not often happen nowadays that a stern parent asks a young man 'his intentions' or objects to a young man speaking to his daughter without having first obtained the father's or guardian's permission. Such things do now and then happen, and are doubtless a survival from the days of 'Mansfield Park' and 'Persuasion.'

CHAPTER XIII

IT seems to me that the majority of good Austenites place 'Emma,' if not at the actual head of the novels, at least on a pinnacle equal to that occupied by 'Pride and Prejudice.' 'Emma' was written, as were 'Mansfield Park' and 'Persuasion,' at Chawton between 1811 and 1816, and 'Emma' was published, as usual anonymously, in 1816. As to my own estimate of it, I must ask, risking monotony, to again distinguish between criticism and opinion. It has to me the attraction, recognised as to a cognate art by Charles Lamb, that it was the first of the novels which I ever read. This was at an age when its subtleties and niceties were perforce beyond my appreciation. Yet its fascination was so great that I read it over and over again, as I have many a time done since. It may, of course, be partly due to recollection of this early glamour that it still seems to me the most uniformly pleasant and sprightly of the novels. There is an air of movement, as well as of fidelity to life, all through it which is irresistible. Emma, with all her pardonable faults, is a most lovable creature, and indeed the only blots upon her character are youthful folly (as in her giving Harriet Smith very bad advice) and that piece of ill-manners to Miss Bates, which one sometimes wishes the author had omitted. In the whole novel there is not one really disagreeable person. There are who think Jane Fairfax delightful. That is a matter of personal taste, but she cannot justly be called disagreeable in the sense wherein the word is used for the present purpose. In 'Pride and Prejudice,' on the other hand, there is more than one disagreeable person. And it is at least open to doubt whether Darcy turned out to be the very pleasantest of husbands. 'Emma' has for me a later, a recent interest. I had what appeared specious reasons for supposing that one character in the book could be more or less identified with an individual original. Those who have the best, or indeed the only real, authority to speak of Miss Austen's views, undeceived me as to this. It has been long known that Miss Austen in general terms disavowed taking, as one may say, portraits from involuntary sitters. It is now known that to this rule she never made an exception, and that nothing could have annoyed her more than a suggestion that Miss Bates or Mr. Collins was a representation of any one individual. All her characters were created—the word is not too strong—from close observation of types, not of any special instance of a type.

This has perhaps been the case with most, if not with all, great novelists. Mr. Thackeray, for instance, in an impressively tragic short story written in his early days, appended a footnote to say that the incidents were taken from life. He said nothing about the characters. People who knew both Mr. Thackeray and Mr. Arcedeckne have written that *Foker* was an obvious caricature of Mr. Arcedeckne, who took his revenge in the most unimpeachable way. But how many attempts have been made to identify characters in that great novelist's works! One set of people are certain that 'the Fotheringay' was meant for Miss X. Another set you will find equally certain that she was meant for Miss Y. There was once a very current identification of George Warrington which was, on the face of it, to any one who knew the identified person, absurd. Need one suppose that Foker was any more an absolute caricature portrait than was the Marquess of Steyne? It is true that a certain illustration of the Marquess in the first edition of 'Vanity Fair' was suppressed and is now scarce. Yet, perhaps, here the author-illustrator's impulse ran away with him. I happened to know intimately the person who unconsciously sat for the face and figure of Major Pendennis. But in the character, long before thought out, there was no likeness to the man who struck Mr. Thackeray as a good type, in physical appearance, for the Major.

What is *certain* about Miss Austen is that she never drew a single character from a single living person. It is said that a very great English novelist sometimes did so. This, again, I feel sure, is a statement that should be largely discounted. No more could Charles Dickens than Miss Austen, whose method was so different from his, have, by mere personal portraiture in writing, turned out so many characters that we recognise as intensely interesting because they are so intensely true and human—or, to sum up in one word, so *alive.*

In 'Emma' surely all the characters, from the leading ones down to the *personæ mutæ*, or nearly *mutæ*, are very much alive. Professor Goldwin Smith holds, as in the case of Sir Walter Elliot, the, as I think, heterodox opinion that 'Mr. Woodhouse's valetudinarianism is perhaps a little overdone,' and in following sentences he goes even much further than this. The explanation of the view taken by Professor Goldwin Smith may possibly be that he never had the fortune or misfortune to meet a real valetudinarian. Those who have encountered such people will see that Mr. Woodhouse is, all things considered, a very pleasant specimen of a curious type, and true to nature in the novelist's sense. That is, he is never disagreeable. He may, one imagines, have been wearisome in actuality just when he is diverting in fiction. But—and this is an important *but*—he never made a slip either from good temper or from good manners. He once offended Mr. John Knightley by a conversation concerning the relative merits of different watering-places.

On this occasion, however, perhaps Mr. John Knightley was in the wrong to take offence at an opinion expressed, however persistently, by one so much his elder. Knightley himself would have let the thing pass, and it is he who with the readiest tact and good breeding rescues the situation. I do not think one can search out a more striking instance of Miss Austen's genius and insight than the finely touched likeness and unlikeness between the brothers Knightley. At every turn of phrase, at every step, so to speak, one knows which is the better man, and yet the point is never pressed by the author. This surely is the excellence of delineation. I cannot recall any precisely similar feat in novel-writing. The thing has been done and well done on the stage, and old playgoers will at once recognise the pieces and performances to which I refer. But there is an important difference. An actor makes an impression which is momentary. When his acting is of the first rank it is remembered by those who 'taste' it as long as they live. But 'litera scripta manet.' If one person says to another 'there was no approaching Mr. Crummles in "Pizarro,"' how can the other, who has not seen that admirable performance, raise any objection? With a book the thing is entirely different. 'Litera scripta manet.' Any one who can read can form his own judgment.

I do not think I am alone in thinking that Emma is the most lovable of Miss Austen's heroines. And after all the best testimony to her merits is that Knightley, a dignified gentleman if ever there was one, loved her for long without avowing his love, and with no restraint upon the fault-finding which Professor Goldwin Smith resents perhaps 'more than reason'. The conditions of social intercourse in that day much more than now admitted reproof, without severity or pedantry, from a man of experience and judgment to a girl with whom, as with her family, he had been long intimately acquainted. And after all it is only on the occasion of Emma's one lapse of good manners to Miss Bates that Knightley speaks to her in real rebuke. The relation between the two characters is throughout consistent. Emma never resents admonition from Knightley. Knightley never hesitates to give it. We are told but little—and this is characteristic of the author—of his feelings, but we are distinctly told that, on a certain occasion, it flashed into Emma's mind that Knightley ought not to marry any one but herself. There is certainly no touch of pettiness in anything that concerns either Emma or Knightley, and no room for anything like the injurious suggestion made by some commentators on 'Pride and Prejudice,' that Eliza Bennet may have been influenced to change her opinions of Darcy by the grandeur of his domain. In the case of Emma and Knightley there was practically no difference either in rank or in fortune, and one feels, with the author, that the match should be made though it was natural enough that Emma should, for a time, be dazzled by the fascinations of Mr. Frank Churchill, who wrote the celebrated 'handsome letter.' So far as Emma and Knightley are concerned all ends as it should. As to Jane Fairfax and Frank Churchill—well, neither of them was quite straightforward, and for that very reason they may have been well suited.

The 'largeness of treatment' in 'Emma' reminds one in an inverse sense of her own description of her work as miniature-painting, a simile, as we have seen, constantly taken up.

The comparison is too modest. A better one might be found in the description by the ingenious Mr. Hardcastle, author of 'Wine and Walnuts,' of a thing invented and perfected by the great scene-painter, Loutherbourg:

'The stage on which the Eidophusikon was represented was little more than six feet wide, and about eight feet in depth ; yet such was the painter's knowledge of effect and scientific arrangement, and the scenes which he described were so completely illusive, that the space appeared to recede for many miles, and his horizon seemed as palpably distant from the eye, as the extreme termination of the view would appear in nature.'

CHAPTER XIV

CONCERNING 'The Watsons' and 'Lady Susan,' and especially concerning 'Lady Susan' because it is a completed work and not, like 'The Watsons,' the beginning of a book which might, or might not, if and when finished, have ranked with the author's best achievements. This work does not appear in the latest edition of Miss Austen's novels, possibly for copyright reasons. Therefore I have not the great advantage of comparing my own estimate of it with that of Mr. Austin Dobson. Professor Goldwin Smith however has written with no uncertainty about it. It is a perilous or at least a very venturous task to put one's own opinion against the deliberate judgment of so fine and expert a critic as Professor Goldwin Smith. Yet, with all deference to those attainments which have so justly earned for him a great name, I cannot but disagree with him as to 'Lady Susan.' He brings against it an indictment powerfully, of course, worded and obviously well thought out. He describes it as a work which might have been written by 'a Parisian novelist'—meaning thereby a Parisian novelist of the worser school. It is true, as he infers, that the character of 'Lady Susan' herself is about as disagreeable—one might say odious—as a character can be. But is a great novelist to be restricted to charming and virtuous heroines? Shall we refuse to admire the depiction of Miss Becky Sharp because she was not a model of propriety? Are we to ignore the skill in character-drawing in 'Lady Susan' because Fanny Price and Emma Woodhouse are far more agreeable women? It is difficult to avoid the supposition that 'Lady Susan' has been underrated just because it is the only book in which Miss Austen deliberately drew the character of a thorough scoundrel—a female scoundrel, the most difficult kind of rogue to portray accurately.

The book is not a pleasant book. It was not meant to be. Was Iago meant to be pleasant to the reader or spectator of 'Othello'? He was, according to a great critic, 'a comfortable careless villain,' and his chief companions in the play take him, each in his own way, for an excellent companion. Lady Susan is, it seems to me, compact, so far as a woman can be, of the same kind of stuff that went to make Iago what he was. She was thoroughly unburdened with scruples. She did, now and then, a little good that a great harm might come. She distrusted everybody, knowing that at any moment she might find that everybody distrusted her. She was as limited in foresight as any evil-minded creature that any historian or writer of fiction (and the two callings are sometimes united) has ever put on paper. She was an adroit rogue, perhaps even more adroit than

Becky Sharp, and yet she defeated herself. All the more was she distinct from the kind of character that Professor Goldwin Smith may possibly have had in his mind when he referred to French novels. If, to take an instance not yet antique, M. Gaboriau dealt with an adventuress, he sometimes brought her out scatheless as well as shameless. Miss Austen, judiciously as always, leaves her readers to form their own conclusions as to Lady Susan's future of happiness or the reverse. This must be but conjecture. The author has drawn with a skill all her own the character of a woman to be avoided, and a woman who has been enough 'found out' to make it doubtful if she will ever 'make her way' again. Still, it is left doubtful, and might well be doubtful—Lady Susan was a very clever woman.

The book is written in a form that is not very popular now, that of interchanged letters. Yet I think that it is not so much this as the novel's unlikeness to all Miss Austen's other works that has endued it with a less popularity. It seems to me that here she showed beyond doubt that, if she liked, she could do 'the big bow-wow' of which Sir Walter Scott wrote. And is it too curious to imagine that just because he was so much to the front she deliberately adopted another style? There is some ground for this possibly fantastic supposition in an often-quoted passage wherein Miss Austen, in her vein of playful irony, observed that Sir Walter Scott should be content with the fame of his poems and leave the field of prose fiction clear to others. However, this is but the merest supposition or imagination as to what may or may not have influenced Miss Austen in choosing for herself a method and style which remain practically unique. Mrs. Inchbald, Miss Mitford, and in later days Mrs. Gaskell worked with success upon the same kind of material which was favourite to Miss Austen, but the success in each case was of a different kind. Miss Austen's style, whatever she may have learnt by avoidance of faults in other writers—there was certainly no question of imitation—was a thing by itself, a thing due to the genius which she was the last of people to appreciate.

'The Watsons,' as the unfinished work is called, was written—as Mr. Austen Leigh discovered from watermarks on the pages of the manuscript—while Miss Austen was staying at Bath. As a matter of criticism on a fragment there is, I think, nothing to be added to what Mr. Austen Leigh says, that 'it is certain that the mine at which she had long laboured was not worked out, and that she was still diligently employed in collecting fresh materials from it.'

For 'Lady Susan' there seems to be no actually assignable date. It was supposed by the family to be 'an early production,' and this gives perhaps some colour to my suggestion as to the subsequent change in style.

It was in 1817 that Miss Austen, who had been ailing for some time, found herself seriously ill and moved from Chawton to Winchester, where, in spite of all that medical science could do, she breathed her last on July 18th.

At the moment of writing I hear with utmost pleasure of a scheme for a memorial painted window in Winchester Cathedral. Meanwhile, there could surely be no better text, no better comment on her life than the words chosen by Mr. Austen Leigh from the last chapter of Proverbs for the tablet put up in her memory in the Cathedral: 'She openeth her mouth with wisdom; and in her tongue is the law of kindness.'

FINIS